A Streetcar Named Desire

BESTSELLING FICTION

- 1984 by George Orwell
  Fiction/Classics, ISBN: 9788193545836
- Animal Farm by George Orwell
  Fiction/Classics, ISBN: 9789387669062
- Anthem by Ayn Rand
  Fiction/Classics, ISBN: 9789389157178
- As a Man Thinketh by James Allen
  Fiction/Classics, ISBN: 9789388118422
- Demian by Hermann Hesse
  Fiction/Classics, ISBN: 9789388118170
- Gitanjali by Rabindranath Tagore
  Fiction/Poems, ISBN: 9789387669079
- Mansarover 1 (Hindi) by Premchand
  Fiction/Short Stories, ISBN: 9789387669086
- Selected Stories of Rabindranath Tagore by Tagore
  Fiction/Short Stories, ISBN: 9789387669307
- Siddhartha by Hermann Hesse
  Fiction/Classics, ISBN: 9789387669116
- Tales from India by Rudyard Kipling
  Fiction/Short Stories, ISBN: 9789387669123
- Tales from Shakespeare by Charles Lamb, Mary Lamb
  Fiction/Short Stories, ISBN: 9789387669314
- The Jungle Book by Rudyard Kipling
  Children's/Classics, ISBN: 9789387669338
- The Light of Asia by Sir Edwin Arnold
  Fiction/Poetry, ISBN: 9789387669130
- The Prophet by Kahlil Gibran
  Fiction/Classics, ISBN: 9789388118453

Search the book by its ISBN

A Streetcar Named Desire

One Last Chance at Love...

Tennessee Williams

GENERAL PRESS

Published by

GENERAL PRESS

4805/24, Fourth Floor, Krishna House
Ansari Road, Daryaganj, New Delhi - 110002
Ph : 011-23282971, 45795759
E-mail : generalpressindia@gmail.com

www.generalpress.in

First Edition : 2022

ISBN : 9789354991493

Published by Azeem Ahmad Khan for General Press

Contents

The Characters

Blanche

Stella

Stanley

Mitch

Eunice

Steve

Pablo

A Negro Woman

A Doctor

A Nurse

A Young Collector

A Mexican Woman

Scene 1

The exterior of a two-story corner building on a street in New Orleans which is named Elysian Fields and runs between the L & N tracks and the river. The section is poor but, unlike corresponding sections in other American cities, it has a raffish charm. The houses are mostly white frame, weathered gray, with rickety outside stairs and galleries and quaintly ornamented gables. This building contains two flats, upstairs and down. Faded white stairs ascend to the entrances of both.

It is first dark of an evening early in May. The sky that shows around the dim white building is a peculiarly tender blue, almost a turquoise, which invests the scene with a kind of lyricism and gracefully attenuates the atmosphere of decay. You can almost feel the warm breath of the brown river beyond the river warehouses with their faint redolences of bananas and coffee. A corresponding air is evoked by the music of Negro entertainers at a barroom around the corner. In this part of New Orleans you are practically always just around the corner, or a few doors down the street, from a tinny piano being played with the infatuated fluency of brown fingers. This "Blue Piano" expresses the spirit of the life which goes on here.

Two women, one white and one colored, are taking the air on the steps of the building. The white woman is Eunice, who occupies the upstairs flat; the colored woman a neighbor, for New Orleans is a cosmopolitan city where there is a relatively warm and easy intermingling of races in the old part of town.

Above the music of the "Blue Piano" the voices of people on the street can be heard overlapping.

* * *

[*Two men come around the corner, Stanley Kowalski and Mitch. They are about twenty-eight or thirty years old, roughly dressed in blue denim work clothes. Stanley carries his bowling jacket and a red-stained package from a butcher's. They stop at the foot of the steps.*]

STANLEY : [*bellowing*] Hey, there! Stella, Baby!

[*Stella comes out on the first floor landing, a gentle young woman, about twenty-five, and of a background obviously quite different from her husband's.*]

STELLA : [*mildly*] Don't holler at me like that. Hi, Mitch.

STANLEY : Catch!

STELLA : What?

STANLEY : Meat!

[*Be heaves the package at her. She cries out in protest but manages to catch it; then she laughes breathlessly. Her husband and his companion have already started back around the comer.*]

STELLA : [*calling after him*] Stanley! Where are you going?

STANLEY : Bowling!

STELLA : Can I come watch?

STANLEY : Come on. [*He goes out.*]

STELLA : Be over soon. [*To the white woman*] Hello, Eunice. How are you?

EUNICE : I'm all right. Tell Steve to get him a poor boy's sandwich 'cause nothing's left here.

[*They all laugh; the colored woman does not stop. Stella goes out.*]

COLORED W.: What was that package he th'ew at 'er? [*She rises from steps, laughing louder.*]

EUNICE : You hush, now!

NEGRO W. : Catch *what*!

[*She continues to laugh. Blanche comes around the corner, currying a valise. She looks at a slip of paper, then at the building, then again at the slip and again at the building. Her expression is one of shocked disbelief. Her appearance is incongruous to this setting. She is daintily dressed in a white suit with a fluffy bodice, necklace and earrings of pearl, white gloves and hat, looking as if she were arriving at a summer tea or cocktail party in the garden district. She is about five years older than Stella. Her delicate beauty must avoid a strong light. There is something about her uncertain manner, as well as her white clothes, that suggests a moth.*]

EUNICE : [*finally*] What's the matter, honey? Are you lost?

BLANCHE : [*with faintly hysterical humor*] They told me to take a streetcar named Desire, and then transfer to one called Cemeteries and ride six blocks and get off at—Elysian Fields!

EUNICE : That's where you are now.

BLANCHE : At Elysian Fields?

EUNICE : This here is Elysian Fields.

BLANCHE : They mustn't have understood what number I wanted.

EUNICE : What number you lookin' for?

[*Blanche wearily refers to the slip of paper.*]

BLANCHE : Six thirty-two.

EUNICE : You don't have to look no further.

BLANCHE : [*uncomprehendingly*] I'm looking for my sister, Stella DuBois. I mean—Mrs. Stanley Kowalski.

EUNICE : That's the party.—You just did miss her, though.

BLANCHE : This—can this be—her home?

EUNICE : She's got the downstairs here and I got the up.

BLANCHE : Oh. She's—out?

EUNICE : You noticed that bowling alley around the corner?

BLANCHE : I'm—not sure I did.

EUNICE : Well, that's where she's at, watchin' her husband bowl. [*There is a pause*] You want to leave your suitcase here an' go find her?

BLANCHE : No.

NEGRO W. : I'll go tell her you come.

BLANCHE : Thanks.

NEGRO W. : You welcome. [*She goes out.*]

EUNICE : She wasn't expecting you?

BLANCHE : No. No, not tonight.

EUNICE : Well, why don't you just go in and make yourself at home till they get back.

BLANCHE : How could I—do that?

EUNICE : We own this place so I can let you in.

[*She gets up and opens the downstairs door. A light goes on behind the blind, turning it light blue. Blanche slowly follows her into the downstairs flat. The surrounding areas dim out as the interior is lighted.*]

[*Two rooms can be seen, not too clearly defined. The one first entered is primarily a kitchen but contains a folding bed to be used by Blanche. The room beyond this is a bedroom. Off this room is a narrow door to a bathroom.*]

EUNICE : [*defensively, noticing Blanche's look*] It's sort of messed up right now but when it's clean it's real sweet.

BLANCHE : Is it?

EUNICE : Uh, huh, I think so. So you're Stella's sister?

BLANCHE : Yes. [*Wanting to get rid of her*] Thanks for letting me in.

EUNICE : *Por nada*, as the Mexicans say, *por nada*! Stella spoke of you.

BLANCHE : Yes?

EUNICE : I think she said you taught school.

BLANCHE : Yes.

EUNICE : And you're from Mississippi, huh?

BLANCHE : Yes.

EUNICE : She showed me a picture of your home-place, the plantation.

BLANCHE : Belle Reve?

EUNICE : A great big place with white columns.

BLANCHE : Yes...

EUNICE : A place like that must be awful hard to keep up.

BLANCHE : If you will excuse me. I'm just about to drop.

EUNICE : Sure, honey. Why don't you set down?

BLANCHE : What I meant was I'd like to be left alone.

EUNICE : Aw. I'll make myself scarce, in that case.

BLANCHE : I didn't mean to be rude, but—

EUNICE : I'll drop by the bowling alley an' hustle her up. [*She goes out the door.*]

[*Blanche sits in a chair very stiffly with her shoulders slightly hunched and her legs pressed close together and her hands tightly clutching her purse as if she were quite cold. After a while the blind look goes out of her eyes and she begins to look slowly around. A cat screeches. She catches her breath with a startled gesture. Suddenly she notices something in a half-opened closet. She springs up and crosses to it, and removes a whiskey bottle. She pours a half tumbler of whiskey and tosses it down. She carefully replaces the bottle and washes out the tumbler at the sink. Then she resumes her seat in front of the table.*]

BLANCHE : [*faintly to herself*] I've got to keep hold of myself!

[*Stella comes quickly around the corner of the building and runs to the door of the downstairs flat.*]

STELLA : [*calling out joyfully*] Blanche!

[*For a moment they stare at each other. Then Blanche springs up and runs to her with a wild cry.*]

BLANCHE : Stella, oh, Stella, Stella! Stella for Star!

[*She begins to speak with feverish vivacity as if she feared for either of them to stop and think. They catch each other in a spasmodic embrace.*]

BLANCHE : Now, then, let me look at you. But don't you look at me, Stella, no, no, no, not till later, not till I've bathed and rested! And turn that over-light off! Turn that off! I won't be looked at in this merciless glare! [*Stella laughs and complies*] Come back here now! Oh, my baby! Stella! Stella for Star! [*She embraces her again*] I thought you would never come back to this horrible place! What am I saying? I didn't mean to say that. I meant to be nice about it and say—Oh, what a convenient location and such—Haa-ha! Precious lamb! You haven't said a *word* to me.

STELLA : You haven't given me a chance to, honey! [*She laughs, but her glance at Blanche is a little anxious.*]

BLANCHE : Well, now you talk. Open your pretty mouth and talk while I look around for some liquor! I know you must have some liquor on the place! Where could it be, I wonder? Oh, I spy, I spy!

[*She rushes to the closet and removes the bottle; she is shaking all over and panting for breath as she tries to laugh. The bottle nearly slips from her grasp.*]

STELLA : [*noticing*] Blanche, you sit down and let me pour the drinks. I don't know what we've got to mix with. Maybe a coke's in the icebox. Look'n see, honey, while I'm—

BLANCHE : No coke, honey, not with my nerves tonight! Where—where—where is—?

STELLA : Stanley? Bowling! He loves it. They're having a—found some soda!—tournament…

BLANCHE : Just water, baby, to chase it! Now don't get worried, your sister hasn't turned into a drunkard, she's just all shaken up and hot and tired and dirty! You sit down, now, and explain this place to me! What are you doing in a place like this?

STELLA : Now, Blanche—

BLANCHE : Oh, I'm not going to be hypocritical, I'm going to be honestly critical about it! Never, never, never in my worst dreams could I picture—Only Poe! Only Mr. Edgar Allan Poe!—could do it justice! Out there I suppose is the ghoul-haunted woodland of Weir! [*She laughs.*]

STELLA : No, honey, those are the L & N tracks.

BLANCHE : No, now seriously, putting joking aside. Why didn't you tell me, why didn't you write me, honey, why didn't you let me know?

STELLA : [*carefully, pouring herself a drink*] Tell you what, Blanche?

BLANCHE : Why, that you had to live in these conditions!

STELLA : Aren't you being a little intense about it? It's not that bad at all! New Orleans isn't like other cities.

BLANCHE : This has got nothing to do with New Orleans. You might as well say—forgive me, blessed baby! [*She suddenly stops short*] The subject is closed!

STELLA : [*a little drily*] Thanks.

[*During the pause, Blanche stares at her. She smiles at Blanche.*]

BLANCHE : [*looking down at her glass, which shakes in her hand*] You're all I've got in the world, and you're not glad to see me!

STELLA : [*sincerely*] Why, Blanche, you know that's not true.

BLANCHE : No?—I'd forgotten how quiet you were.

STELLA : You never did give me a chance to say much, Blanche. So I just got in the habit of being quiet around you.

BLANCHE : [*vaguely*] A good habit to get into… [*then, abruptly*] You haven't asked me how I happened to get away from the school before the spring term ended.

STELLA : Well, I thought you'd volunteer that information—if you wanted to tell me.

BLANCHE : You thought I'd been fired?

STELLA : No, I—thought you might have—resigned…

BLANCHE : I was so exhausted by all I'd been through my—nerves broke. [*Nervously tamping cigarette*] I was on the verge of—lunacy, almost! So Mr. Graves—Mr. Graves is the high school superintendent—he suggested I take a leave of absence. I couldn't put all of those details into the wire… [*She drinks quickly*] Oh, this buzzes right through me and feels so *good!*

STELLA : Won't you have another?

BLANCHE : No, one's my limit.

STELLA : Sure?

BLANCHE : You haven't said a word about my appearance.

STELLA : You look just fine.

BLANCHE : God love you for a liar! Daylight never exposed so total a ruin! But you—you've put on some weight, yes, you're just as plump as a little partridge! And it's so becoming to you!

STELLA : Now, Blanche—

BLANCHE : Yes, it is, it is or I wouldn't say it! You just have to watch around the hips a little. Stand up.

STELLA : Not now.

BLANCHE : You hear me? I said stand up! [*Stella complies reluctantly*] You messy child, you, you've spilt something on the pretty white lace collar! About your hair—you ought to have it cut in a feather bob with your dainty features. Stella, you have a maid, don't you?

STELLA : No. With only two rooms it's—

BLANCHE : What? *Two* rooms, did you say?

STELLA : This one and—[*She is embarrassed.*]

BLANCHE : The other one? [*She laughs sharply. There is an embarrassed silence.*]

BLANCHE : I am going to take just one little tiny nip more, sort of to put the stopper on, so to speak... Then put the bottle away so I won't be tempted. [*She rises*] I want you to look at my figure! [*She turns around*] You know I haven't put on one ounce in ten years, Stella? I weigh what I weighed the summer you left Belle Reve. The summer Dad died and you left us...

STELLA : [*a little wearily*] It's just incredible, Blanche, how well you're looking.

BLANCHE : [*They both laugh uncomfortably*] But, Stella, there's only two rooms, I don't see where you're going to put me!

STELLA : We're going to put you in here.

BLANCHE : What kind of bed's this—one of those collapsible things? [*She sits on it.*]

STELLA : Does it feel all right?

BLANCHE : [*dubiously*] Wonderful, honey. I don't like a bed that gives much. But there's no door between the two rooms, and Stanley—will it be decent?

STELLA : Stanley is Polish, you know.

BLANCHE : Oh, yes. They're something like Irish, aren't they?

STELLA : Well—

BLANCHE : Only not so—highbrow? [*They both laugh again in the same way.*] I brought some nice clothes to meet all your lovely friends in.

STELLA : I'm afraid you won't think they are lovely.

BLANCHE : What are they like?

STELLA : They're Stanley's friends.

BLANCHE : Polacks?

STELLA : They're a mixed lot, Blanche.

BLANCHE : Heterogeneous—types?

STELLA : Oh, yes. Yes, types is right!

BLANCHE : Well—anyhow—I brought nice clothes and I'll wear them. I guess you're hoping I'll say I'll put up at a hotel, but I'm not going to put up at a hotel. I want to be *near* you, got to be *with* somebody, I can't be *alone*! Because—as you must have noticed—I'm—*not* very *well*… [*Her voice drops and her look is frightened.*]

STELLA : You seem a little bit nervous or overwrought or something.

BLANCHE : Will Stanley like me, or will I just be a visiting in-law, Stella? I couldn't stand that.

STELLA : You'll get along fine together, if you'll just try not to—well—compare him with men that we went out with at home.

BLANCHE : Is he so—different?

STELLA : Yes. A different species.

BLANCHE : In what way; what's he like?

STELLA : Oh, you can't describe someone you're in love with! Here's a picture of him! [*She hands a photograph to Blanche.*]

BLANCHE : An officer?

STELLA : A Master Sergeant in the Engineers' Corps. Those are decorations!

BLANCHE : He had those on when you met him?

STELLA : I assure you I wasn't just blinded by all the brass.

BLANCHE : That's not what I—

STELLA : But of course there were things to adjust myself to later on.

BLANCHE : Such as his civilian background! [*Stella laughs uncertainly*] How did he take it when you said I was coming?

STELLA : Oh, Stanley doesn't know yet.

BLANCHE : [*frightened*] You—haven't told him?

STELLA : He's on the road a good deal.

BLANCHE : Oh. Travels?

STELLA : Yes.

BLANCHE : Good. I mean—isn't it?

STELLA : [*half to herself*] I can hardly stand it when he is away for a night...

BLANCHE : Why, Stella!

STELLA : When he's away for a week I nearly go wild!

BLANCHE : Gracious!

STELLA : And when he comes back I cry on his lap like a baby... [*She smiles to herself.*]

BLANCHE : I guess that is what is meant by being in love... [*Stella looks up with a radiant smile.*] Stella—

STELLA : What?

BLANCHE : [*in an uneasy rush*] I haven't asked you the things you probably thought I was going to ask. And so I'll expect you to be understanding about what *I* have to tell *you*.

STELLA : What, Blanche? [*Her face turns anxious.*]

BLANCHE : Well, Stella—you're going to reproach me, I know that you're bound to reproach me—but before you do—take into consideration—you left! *I* stayed and struggled! You came to New Orleans and looked out for yourself. I stayed at *Belle Reve* and tried to hold it together! I'm not meaning this in any reproachful way, but *all* the burden descended on *my* shoulders.

STELLA : The best I could do was make my own living, Blanche. [*Blanche begins to shake again with intensity.*]

BLANCHE : I know, I know. But you are the one that abandoned Belle Reve, not I! I stayed and fought for it, bled for it, almost died for it!

STELLA : Stop this hysterical outburst and tell me what's happened! What do you mean fought and bled? What kind of—

BLANCHE : I knew you would, Stella. I knew you would take this attitude about it!

STELLA : About—what?—please!

BLANCHE : [*slowly*] The loss—the loss…

STELLA : Belle Reve? Lost, is it? No!

BLANCHE : Yes, Stella.

[*They stare at each other across the yellow-checked linoleum of the table. Blanche slowly nods her head and Stella looks slowly down at her hands folded on the table. The music of the "blue piano" grows louder. Blanche touches her handkerchief to her forehead.*]

STELLA : But how did it go? What happened?

BLANCHE : [*springing up*] You're a fine one to ask me how it went!

STELLA : Blanche!

BLANCHE : You're a fine one to sit there accusing me of it!

STELLA : Blanche!

BLANCHE : I, I, *I* took the blows in my face and my body! All of those deaths! The long parade to the graveyard! Father, mother! Margaret, that dreadful way! So big with it, it couldn't be put in a coffin! But had to be burned like rubbish! You just came home in time for the funerals, Stella. And funerals are pretty compared to deaths. Funerals are quiet, but deaths—not always. Sometimes their breathing is hoarse, and sometimes it rattles, and sometimes they even cry out to you, "Don't let me go!" Even the old, sometimes, say, "Don't let me go." As if you were able to stop them! But funerals are quiet, with pretty flowers. And, oh, what gorgeous boxes they pack them away in! Unless you were there at the bed when they cried out, "Hold me!" you'd never suspect there was the struggle for breath and bleeding. You didn't dream, but I saw! Saw!

Saw! And now you sit there telling me with your eyes that I let the place go! How in hell do you think all that sickness and dying was paid for? Death is expensive, Miss Stella! And old Cousin Jessie's right after Margaret's, hers! Why, the Grim Reaper had put up his tent on our doorstep!... Stella. Belle Reve was his headquarters! Honey—that's how it slipped through my fingers! Which of them left us a fortune? Which of them left a cent of insurance even? Only poor Jessie—one hundred to pay for her coffin. That was all, Stella! And I with my pitiful salary at the school. Yes, accuse me! Sit there and stare at me, thinking I let the place go! I let the place go? Where were you! In bed with your—Polack!

STELLA : [*springing*] Blanche! You be still! That's enough! [*She starts out.*]

BLANCHE : Where are you going?

STELLA : I'm going into the bathroom to wash my face.

BLANCHE : Oh, Stella, Stella, you're crying!

STELLA : Does that surprise you?

BLANCHE : Forgive me—I didn't mean to—

[*The sound of men's voices is heard. Stella goes into the bathroom, closing the door behind her. When the men appear, and Blanche realizes it must be Stanley returning, she moves uncertainly from the bathroom door to the dressing table, looking apprehensively toward the front door. Stanley enters, followed by Steve and Mitch. Stanley pauses near his door, Steve by the foot of the spiral stair, and Mitch is slightly above and to the right of them, about to go out. As the men enter, we hear some of the following dialogue.*]

STANLEY : Is that how he got it?

STEVE : Sure that's how he got it. He hit the old weather-bird for 300 bucks on a six-number-ticket.

MITCH : Don't tell him those things; he'll believe it.

[*Mitch starts out.*]

STANLEY : [*restraining Mitch*] Hey, Mitch-come back here.

[*Blanche, at the sound of voices, retires in the bedroom. She picks up Stanley's photo from dressing table, looks at it, puts it down. When Stanley enters the apartment, she darts and hides behind the screen at the head of bed.*]

STEVE : [*to Stanley and Mitch*] Hey, are we playin' poker tomorrow?

STANLEY : Sure—at Mitch's.

MITCH : [*hearing this, returns quickly to the stair rail*] No—not at my place. My mother's still sick!

STANLEY : Okay, at my place... [*Mitch starts out again*] But you bring the beer!

[*Mitch pretends not to hear,—calls out "Goodnight all," and goes out, singing. Eunice's voice is heard, above:*]

Break it up down there! I made the spaghetti dish and ate it myself.

STEVE : [*going upstairs*] I told you and phoned you we was playing. [*To the men*] Jax beer!

EUNICE : You never phoned me once.

STEVE : I told you at breakfast—and phoned you at lunch...

EUNICE : Well, never mind about that. You just get yourself home here once in a while.

STEVE : You want it in the papers?

[*More laughter and shouts of parting come from the men. Stanley throws the screen door of the kitchen open and comes in. He is of medium height, about five feet eight or nine, and strongly, compactly built. Animal joy in his being is implicit in all his movements and attitudes. Since earliest manhood the center of his life has been pleasure with women, the giving and taking of it, not with weak indulgence, dependency, but with the power and pride of a richly feathered male bird among hens. Branching out from this complete and satisfying center are all the auxiliary channels of his life, such as his heartiness with men, his appreciation of rough humor, his love of good drink and food and games, his car, his radio, everything that is his, that bears his emblem of the gaudy seed-bearer. He sizes women up at a glance, with sexual classifications, crude images flashing into his mind and determining the way he smiles at them.*]

BLANCHE : [*drawing involuntarily back from his stare*] You must be Stanley. I'm Blanche.

STANLEY : Stella's sister?

BLANCHE : Yes.

STANLEY : H'lo. Where's the little woman?

BLANCHE : In the bathroom.

STANLEY : Oh. Didn't know you were coming in town.

BLANCHE : I—uh—

STANLEY : Where you from, Blanche?

BLANCHE : Why, I—live in Laurel.

[*He has crossed to the closet and removed the whiskey bottle.*]

STANLEY : In Laurel, huh? Oh, yeah. Yeah, in Laurel, that's right. Not in my territory. Liquor goes fast in hot weather. [*He holds the bottle to the light to observe its depletion.*] Have a shot?

BLANCHE : No, I—rarely touch it.

STANLEY : Some people rarely touch it, but it touches them often.

BLANCHE : [*faintly*] Ha-ha.

STANLEY : My clothes 're stickin' to me. Do you mind if I make myself comfortable? [*He starts to remove his shirt.*]

BLANCHE : Please, please do.

STANLEY : Be comfortable is my motto.

BLANCHE : It's mine, too. It's hard to stay looking fresh. I haven't washed or even powdered my face and— here you are!

STANLEY : You know you can catch cold sitting around in damp things, especially when you been exercising hard like bowling is. You're a teacher, aren't you?

BLANCHE : Yes.

STANLEY : What do you teach, Blanche?

BLANCHE : English.

STANLEY : I never was a very good English student. How long you here for, Blanche?

BLANCHE : I—don't know yet.

STANLEY : You going to shack up here?

BLANCHE : I thought I would if it's not inconvenient for you all.

STANLEY : Good.

BLANCHE : Traveling wears me out.

STANLEY : Well, take it easy.

[*A cat screeches near the window. Blanche springs up.*]

BLANCHE : What's that?

STANLEY : Cats... Hey, Stella!

STELLA : [*faintly, from the bathroom*] Yes, Stanley.

STANLEY : Haven't fallen in, have you? [*He grins at Blanche. She tries unsuccessfully to smile back. There is a silence*] I'm afraid I'll strike you as being the unrefined type. Stella's spoke of you a good deal. You were married once, weren't you?

[*The music of the polka rises up, faint in the distance.*]

BLANCHE : Yes. When I was quite young.

STANLEY : What happened?

BLANCHE : The boy—the boy died. [*She sinks back down*] I'm afraid I'm-going to be sick!

[*Her head falls on her arms.*]

Scene 2

It is six o'clock the following evening. Blanche is bathing. Stella is completing her toilette. Blanche's dress, a flowered print, is laid out on Stella's bed. Stanley enters the kitchen from outside, leaving the door open on the perpetual "blue piano" around the corner.

STANLEY : What's all this monkey doings?

STELLA : Oh, Stan! [*She jumps up and kisses him which he accepts with lordly composure*] I'm taking Blanche to Galatoire's for supper and then to a show, because it's your pok'r night.

STANLEY : How about my supper, huh? I'm not going to no Galatoire's for supper!

STELLA : I put you a cold plate on ice.

STANLEY : Well, isn't that just dandy!

STELLA : I'm going to try to keep Blanche out till the party breaks up because I don't know how she would take it. So we'll go to one of the little places in the Quarter afterwards and you'd better give me some money.

STANLEY : Where is she?

STELLA : She's soaking in a hot tub to quiet her nerves. She's terribly upset.

STANLEY : Over what?

STELLA : She's been through such an ordeal.

STANLEY : Yeah?

STELLA : Stan, we've—lost Belle Reve!

STANLEY : The place in the country?

STELLA : Yes.

STANLEY : How?

STELLA : [*vaguely*] Oh, it had to be—sacrificed or something. [*There is a pause while Stanley considers. Stella is changing into her dress*] When she comes in be sure to say something nice about her appearance. And, oh! Don't mention the baby. I haven't said anything yet, I'm waiting until she gets in a quieter condition.

STANLEY : [*ominously*] So!

STELLA : And try to understand her and be nice to her, Stan.

BLANCHE : [*singing in the bathroom*]
"From the land of the sky blue water,
They brought a captive maid!"

STELLA : She wasn't expecting to find us in such a small place. You see I'd tried to gloss things over a little in my letters.

STANLEY : So?

STELLA : And admire her dress and tell her she's looking wonderful. That's important with Blanche. Her little weakness!

STANLEY : Yeah. I get the idea. Now let's skip back a little to where you said the country place was disposed of.

STELLA : Oh!—yes…

STANLEY : How about that? Let's have a few more details on that subject.

STELLA : It's best not to talk much about it until she's calmed down.

STANLEY : So that's the deal, huh? Sister Blanche cannot be annoyed with business details right now!

STELLA : You saw how she was last night.

STANLEY : Uh-hum, I saw how she was. Now let's have a gander at the bill of sale.

STELLA : I haven't seen any.

STANLEY : She didn't show you no papers, no deed of sale or nothing like that, huh?

STELLA : It seems like it wasn't sold.

STANLEY : Well what in hell was it then, give away? To charity?

STELLA : Shhh! She'll hear you.

STANLEY : I don't care if she hears me. Let's see the papers!

STELLA : There weren't any papers, she didn't show any papers, I don't care about papers.

STANLEY : Have you ever heard of the Napoleonic code?

STELLA : No, Stanley, I haven't heard of the Napoleonic code, if I have, I don't see what it—

STANLEY : Let me enlighten you on a point or two, baby.

STELLA : Yes?

STANLEY : In the state of Louisiana we have the Napoleonic code according to which what belongs to the wife belongs to the husband and vice versa. For instance if I had a piece of property, or you had a piece of property—

STELLA : My head is swimming!

STANLEY : All right, I'll wait till she gets through soaking in a hot tub and then I'll inquire if she is acquainted with the Napoleonic code. It looks to me like you have been swindled, baby, and when you're swindled under the Napoleonic code I'm swindled too. And I don't like to be swindled.

STELLA : There's plenty of time to ask her questions later but if you do now she'll go to pieces again. I don't understand what happened to Belle Reve but you don't know how ridiculous you are being when you suggest that my sister or I or anyone of our family could have perpetrated a swindle on anyone else.

STANLEY : Then where's the money if the place was sold?

STELLA : Not sold—*lost, lost*!

[*He stalks into bedroom, and she follows him.*]

STELLA : Stanley!

[*He pulls open the wardrobe trunk standing in middle of room and jerks out an armful of dresses.*]

STANLEY : Open your eyes to this stuff! You think she got them out of a teacher's pay?

STELLA : Hush!

STANLEY : Look at these feathers and furs that she come here to preen herself in! What's this here? A solid-gold dress, I believe! And this one! What is these here? Fox-pieces! [*He blows on them.*] Genuine fox fur-pieces, a half a mile long! Where are your fox-pieces, Stella? Bushy snow-white ones, no less! Where are your white fox-pieces?

STELLA : Those are inexpensive summer furs that Blanche has had a long time.

STANLEY : I got an acquaintance who deals in this sort of merchandise. I'll have him in here to appraise it. I'm willing to bet you there's thousands of dollars invested in this stuff here!

STELLA : Don't be such an idiot, Stanley!

[*He hurls the furs on the daybed. Then he jerks open small drawer in the trunk and pulls up a fist-full of costume jewellery.*]

STANLEY : And what have we here? The treasure chest of a pirate!

STELLA : Oh, Stanley!

STANLEY : Pearls! Ropes of them! What is this sister of yours, a deep-sea diver who brings up sunken treasure? Or is she the champion safe-cracker of all time! Bracelets of solid gold, too! Where are your pearls and gold bracelets?

STELLA : Shhh ! Be still, Stanley!

STANLEY : And diamonds! A crown for an empress!

STELLA : A rhinestone tiara she wore to a costume ball.

STANLEY : What's rhinestone?

STELLA : Next door to glass.

STANLEY : Are you kidding? I have an acquaintance that works in a jewellery store. I'll have him in here to make an appraisal of this. Here's your plantation, or what was left of it, here!

STELLA : You have no idea how stupid and horrid you're being! Now close that trunk before she comes out of the bathroom!

[*He kicks the trunk partly closed and sits on the kitchen table.*]

STANLEY : The Kowalskis and the DuBois have different notions.

STELLA : [*angrily*] Indeed they have, thank heavens!—I'm going outside. [*She snatches up her white hat and gloves and crosses to the outside door.*] You come out with me while Blanche is getting dressed.

STANLEY : Since when do you give me orders?

STELLA : Are you going to stay here and insult her?

STANLEY : You're damn tootin' I'm going to stay here.

[*Stella goes out to the porch. Blanche comes out of the bathroom in a red satin robe.*]

BLANCHE : [*airily*] Hello, Stanley! Here I am, all freshly bathed and scented, and feeling like a brand new human being!

[*He lights a cigarette.*]

STANLEY : That's good.

BLANCHE : [*drawing the curtains at the windows*] Excuse me while I slip on my pretty new dress!

STANLEY : Go right ahead, Blanche.

[*She closes the drapes between the rooms.*]

BLANCHE : I understand there's to be a little card party to which we ladies are cordially not invited!

STANLEY : [*ominously*] Yeah?

[*Blanche throws off her robe and slips into a flowered print dress.*]

BLANCHE : Where's Stella?

STANLEY : Out on the porch.

BLANCHE : I'm going to ask a favor of you in a moment.

STANLEY : What could that be, I wonder?

BLANCHE : Some buttons in back! You may enter!

[*He crosses through drapes with a smoldering look.*]

How do I look?

STANLEY : You look all right.

BLANCHE : Many thanks! Now the buttons!

STANLEY : I can't do nothing with them.

BLANCHE : You men with your big clumsy fingers. May I have a drag on your cig?

STANLEY : Have one for yourself.

BLANCHE : Why, thanks!... It looks like my trunk has exploded.

STANLEY : Me an' Stella were helping you unpack.

BLANCHE : Well, you certainly did a fast and thorough job of it!

STANLEY : It looks like you raided some stylish shops in Paris.

BLANCHE : Ha-ha! Yes—clothes are my passion!

STANLEY : What does it cost for a string of fur-pieces like that?

BLANCHE : Why, those were a tribute from an admirer of mine!

STANLEY : He must have had a lot of—admiration!

BLANCHE : Oh, in my youth I excited some admiration. But look at me now! [*She smiles at him radiantly*] Would you think it possible that I was once considered to be—attractive?

STANLEY : Your looks are okay.

BLANCHE : I was fishing for a compliment, Stanley.

STANLEY : I don't go in for that stuff.

BLANCHE : What—stuff?

STANLEY : Compliments to women about their looks. I never met a woman that didn't know if she was good-looking or not without being told, and some of them give themselves credit for more than they've got. I once went out with a doll who said to me, "I am the glamorous type, I am the glamorous type!" I said, "So what?"

BLANCHE : And what did she say then?

STANLEY : She didn't say nothing. That shut her up like a clam.

BLANCHE : Did it end the romance?

STANLEY : It ended the conversation—that was all. Some men are took in by this Hollywood glamor stuff and some men are not.

BLANCHE : I'm sure you belong in the second category.

STANLEY : That's right.

BLANCHE : I cannot imagine any witch of a woman casting a spell over you.

STANLEY : That's right.

BLANCHE : You're simple, straightforward and honest, a little bit on the primitive side I should think. To interest you a woman would have to—[*She pauses with an indefinite gesture.*]

STANLEY : [*slowly*] Lay... her cards on the table.

BLANCHE : [*smiling*] Well, I never cared for wishy-washy people. That was why, when you walked in here last night, I said to myself—"My sister has married a man!"—Of course that was all that I could tell about you.

STANLEY : [*booming*] Now let's cut the re-bop?

BLANCHE : [*pressing hands to her ears*] Ouuuuu!

STELLA : [*calling from the steps*] Stanley! You come out here and let Blanche finish dressing!

BLANCHE : I'm through dressing, honey.

STELLA : Well, you come out, then.

STANLEY : Your sister and I are having a little talk.

BLANCHE : [*lightly*] Honey, do me a favor. Run to the drugstore and get me a lemon-coke with plenty of chipped ice in it!—Will you do that for me, Sweetie?

STELLA : [*uncertainly*] Yes. [*She goes around the corner of the building.*]

BLANCHE : The poor little thing was out there listening to us, and I have an idea she doesn't understand you as well as I do... All right; now, Mr. Kowalski, let us proceed without any more double-talk. I'm ready to answer all questions. I've nothing to hide. What is it?

STANLEY : There is such a thing in this state of Louisiana as the Napoleonic code, according to which whatever belongs to my wife is also mine—and vice versa.

BLANCHE : My, but you have an impressive judicial air!

[*She sprays herself with her atomizer; then playfully sprays him with it. He seizes the atomizer and slams it down on the dresser. She throws back her head and laughs.*]

STANLEY : If I didn't know that you was my wife's sister I'd get ideas about you!

BLANCHE : Such as what!

STANLEY : Don't play so dumb. You know what!

BLANCHE : [*she puts the atomizer on the table*] All right. Cards on the table. That suits me. [*She turns to Stanley.*] I know I fib a good deal. After all, a woman's charm is fifty percent illusion, but when a thing is important I tell the truth, and this is the truth: I haven't cheated my sister or you or anyone else as long as I have lived.

STANLEY : Where's the papers? In the trunk?

BLANCHE : Everything that I own is in that trunk.

[*Stanley crosses to the trunk, shoves it roughly open and begins to open compartments.*]

BLANCHE : What in the name of heaven are you thinking of! What's in the back of that little boy's mind of yours? That I am absconding with something, attempting some kind of treachery on my sister?—Let me do that! It will be faster and simpler… [*She crosses to the trunk and takes out a box*] I keep my papers mostly in this tin box. [*She opens it.*]

STANLEY : What's them underneath? [*He indicates another sheaf of papers.*]

BLANCHE : These are love-letters, yellowing with antiquity, all from one boy. [*He snatches them up. She speaks fiercely*] Give those back to me!

STANLEY : I'll have a look at them first!

BLANCHE : The touch of your hands insults them!

STANLEY : Don't pull that stuff!

[*He rips off the ribbon and starts to examine them. Blanche snatches them from him, and they cascade to the floor.*]

BLANCHE : Now that you've touched them I'll burn them!

STANLEY : [*staring, baffled*] What in hell are they?

BLANCHE : [*on the floor gathering them up*] Poems a dead boy wrote. I hurt him the way that you would like to hurt me, but you can't! I'm not young and vulnerable any more. But my young husband was and I—never mind about that! Just give them back to me!

STANLEY : What do you mean by saying you'll have to burn them?

BLANCHE : I'm sorry, I must have lost my head for a moment. Everyone has something he won't let others touch because of their—intimate nature…

[*She now seems faint with exhaustion and she sits down with the strong box and puts on a pair of glasses and goes methodically through a large stack of papers.*]

Ambler & Ambler. Hmmmmm… Crabtree... More Ambler & Ambler.

STANLEY : What is Ambler & Ambler?

BLANCHE : A firm that made loans on the place.

STANLEY : Then it was lost on a mortgage?

BLANCHE : [*touching her forehead*]That must've been what happened.

STANLEY : I don't want no ifs, ands or buts! What's all the rest of them papers?

[*She hands him the entire box. He carries it to the table and starts to examine the papers.*]

BLANCHE : [*picking up a large envelope containing more papers*] There are thousands of papers, stretching back over hundreds of years, affecting Belle Reve as, piece by piece, our improvident grandfathers and father and uncles and brothers exchanged the land for their epic fornications—to put it plainly! [*She removes her glasses with an exhausted laugh*] The four-letter word deprived us of our plantation, till finally all that was left—and Stella can verify that!—was the house itself and about twenty acres of ground, including a graveyard, to which now all but Stella and I have retreated. [*She pours the contents of the envelope on the table*] Here all of them are, all papers! I hereby endow you with them! Take them, peruse them—commit them to memory, even! I think it's wonderfully fitting that Belle Reve should finally be this bunch of old papers in your big, capable hands!... I wonder if Stella's come back with my lemon-coke... [*She leans back and closes her eyes.*]

STANLEY : I have a lawyer acquaintance who will study these out.

BLANCHE : Present them to him with a box of aspirin tablets.

STANLEY : [*becoming somewhat sheepish*] You see, under the Napolconic code—a man has to take an interest in his wife's affairs—especially now that she's going to have a baby.

[*Blanche opens her eyes. The "blue piano" sounds louder.*]

BLANCHE : Stella? Stella going to have a baby? [*dreamily*] I didn't know she was going to have a baby!

[*She gets up and crosses to the outside door. Stella appears around the corner with a carton from the drugstore.*]

[*Stanley goes into the bedroom with the envelope and the box.*]

[*The inner rooms fade to darkness and the outside wall of the house is visible. Blanche meets Stella at the foot of the steps to the sidewalk.*]

BLANCHE : Stella, Stella for star! How lovely to have a baby! It's all right. Everything's all right.

STELLA : I'm sorry he did that to you.

BLANCHE : Oh, I guess he's just not the type that goes for jasmine perfume, but maybe he's what we need to mix with our blood now that we've lost Belle Reve. We thrashed it out. I feel a bit shaky, but I think I handled it nicely, I laughed and treated it all as a joke. [*Steve and Pablo appear, carrying a case of beer.*] I called him a little boy and laughed and flirted. Yes, I was flirting with your husband! [*as the men approach*] The guests are gathering for the poker party.

[*The two men pass between them, and enter the house.*]

Which way do we go now, Stella—this way?

STELLA : No, this way. [*She leads Blanche away.*]

BLANCHE : [*laughing*] The blind are leading the blind!

[*A tamale vendor is heard calling.*]

VENDOR'S VOICE : Red-hot!

Scene 3

The Poker Night

There is a picture of Van Gogh's of a billiard-parlor at night. The kitchen now suggests that sort of lurid nocturnal brilliance, the raw colors of childhood's spectrum. Over the yellow linoleum of the kitchen table hangs an electric bulb with a vivid green glass shade.

The poker players—Stanley, Steve, Mitch and Pablo—wear colored shirts, solid blues, a purple, a red-and-white check, a light green, and they are men at the peak of their physical manhood, as coarse and direct and powerful as the primary colors. There are vivid slices of watermelon on the table, whiskey bottles and glasses. The bedroom is relatively dim with only the light that spills between the portieres and through the wide window on the street. For a moment, there is absorbed silence as a hand is dealt.

STEVE : Anything wild this deal?

PABLO : One-eyed jacks are wild.

STEVE : Give me two cards.

PABLO : You, Mitch?

MITCH : I'm out

PABLO : One.

MITCH : Anyone want a shot?

STANLEY : Yeah. Me.

PABLO : Why don't somebody go to the Chinaman's and bring back a load of chop suey?

STANLEY : When I'm losing you want to eat! Ante up! Openers? Openers! Get y'r ass off the table, Mitch. Nothing belongs on a poker table but cards, chips and whiskey. [*He lurches up and tosses some watermelon rinds to the floor.*]

MITCH : Kind of on your high horse, ain't you?

STANLEY : How many?

STEVE : Give me three.

STANLEY : One.

MITCH : I'm out again. I oughta go home pretty soon.

STANLEY : Shut up.

MITCH : I gotta sick mother. She don't go to sleep until I come in at night.

STANLEY : Then why don't you stay home with her?

MITCH : She says to go out, so I go, but I don't enjoy it. All the while I keep wondering how she is.

STANLEY : Aw, for the sake of Jesus, go home, then!

PABLO : What've you got?

STANLEY : Spade flush.

MITCH : You all are married. But I'll be alone when she goes.—I'm going to the bathroom.

STANLEY : Hurry back and well fix you a sugar-tit.

MITCH : Aw, go rut. [*He crosses through the bedroom into the bathroom.*]

STEVE : [*dealing a hand*] Seven-card stud. [*Telling his joke as he deals*] This ole farmer is out in back of his house sittin' down th'owing corn to the chickens when all at once he hears a loud cackle and this young hen comes lickety split around the side of the house with the rooster right behind her and gaining on her fast.

STANLEY : [*impatient with the story*] Deal!

STEVE : But when the rooster catches sight of the farmer th'owing the corn he puts on the brakes and lets the hen get away and starts pecking corn. And the old farmer says, "Lord God, I hopes I never gits that hungry!"

[*Steve and Pablo laugh. The sisters appear around the corner of the building*]

STELLA : The game is still going on.

BLANCHE : How do I look?

STELLA : Lovely, Blanche.

BLANCHE : I feel so hot and frazzled. Wait till I powder before you open the door. Do I look done in?

STELLA : Why no. You are as fresh as a daisy.

BLANCHE : One that's been picked a few days.

[*Stella opens the door and they enter.*]

STELLA : Well, well, well. I see you boys are still at it!

STANLEY : Where you been?

STELLA : Blanche and I took in a show. Blanche, this is Mr. Gonzales and Mr. Hubbell.

BLANCHE : Please don't get up.

STANLEY : Nobody's going to get up, so don't be worried.

STELLA : How much longer is this game going to continue?

STANLEY : Till we get ready to quit.

BLANCHE : Poker is so fascinating. Could I kibitz?

STANLEY : You could not. Why don't you women go up and sit with Eunice?

STELLA : Because it is nearly two-thirty. [*Blanche crosses into the bedroom and partially closes the portieres*] Couldn't you call it quits after one more hand?

[*A chair scrapes. Stanley gives a loud whack of his hand on her thigh.*]

STELLA : [*sharply*] That's not fun, Stanley.

[*The men laugh. Stella goes into the bedroom.*]

STELLA : It makes me so mad when he does that in front of people.

BLANCHE : I think I will bathe.

STELLA : Again?

BLANCHE : My nerves are in knots. Is the bathroom occupied?

STELLA : I don't know.

[*Blanche knocks. Mitch opens the door and comes out, still wiping his hands on a towel.*]

BLANCHE : Oh!—good evening.

MITCH : Hello. [*He stares at her.*]

STELLA : Blanche, this is Harold Mitchell. My sister, Blanche DuBois.

MITCH : [*with awkward courtesy*] How do you do, Miss DuBois?

STELLA : How is your mother now, Mitch?

MITCH : About the same, thanks. She appreciated your sending over that custard.—Excuse me, please.

[*He crosses slowly back into the kitchen, glancing back at Blanche and coughing a little shyly. He realizes he still has the towel in his hands and with an embarrassed laugh hands it to Stella. Blanche looks after him with a certain interest.*]

BLANCHE : That one seems-superior to the others.

STELLA : Yes, he is.

BLANCHE : I thought he had a sort of sensitive look.

STELLA : His mother is sick.

BLANCHE : Is he married?

STELLA : No.

BLANCHE : Is he a wolf?

STELLA : Why, Blanche! [*Blanche laughs.*] I don't think he would be.

BLANCHE : What does—what does he do?

[*She is unbuttoning her blouse.*]

STELLA : He's on the precision bench in the spare parts department at the plant Stanley travels for.

BLANCHE : Is that something much?

STELLA : No. Stanley's the only one of his crowd that's likely to get anywhere.

BLANCHE : What makes you think Stanley will?

STELLA : Look at him.

BLANCHE : I've looked at him.

STELLA : Then you should know.

BLANCHE : I'm sorry, but I haven't noticed the stamp of genius even on Stanley's forehead.

[*She takes off the blouse and stands in her pink silk brassiere and white skirt in the light through the portieres. The game has continued in undertones.*]

STELLA : It isn't on his forehead and it isn't genius.

BLANCHE : Oh. Well, what is it, and where? I would like to know.

STELLA : It's a drive that he has. You're standing in the light, Blanche!

BLANCHE : Oh, am I!

[*She moves out of the yellow streak of light. Stella has removed her dress and put on a tight blue satin kimono.*]

STELLA : [*with girlish laughter*] You ought to see their wives.

BLANCHE : [*laughingly*] I can imagine. Big, beefy things, I suppose.

STELLA : You know that one upstairs? [*More laughter*] One time [*laughing*] the plaster—[*laughing*] cracked—

STANLEY : You hens cut out that conversation in there!

STELLA : You can't hear us.

STANLEY : Well, you can hear me and I said to hush up!

STELLA : This is my house and I'll talk as much as I want to!

BLANCHE : Stella, don't start a row.

STELLA : He's half drunk!—I'll be out in a minute.

[*She goes into the bathroom. Blanche rises and crosses leisurely to a small white radio and turns it on.*]

STANLEY : Awright, Mitch, you in?

MITCH : What? Oh!—No, I'm out!

[*Blanche moves back into the streak of light. She raises her arms and stretches, as she moves indolently back to the chair. Rhumba music comes over the radio. Mitch rises at the table.*]

STANLEY : Who turned that on in there?

BLANCHE : I did. Do you mind?

STANLEY : Turn it off!

STEVE : Aw, let the girls have their music.

PABLO : Sure, that's good, leave it on!

STEVE : Sounds like Xavier Cugat!

[*Stanley jumps up and, crossing to the radio, turns it off. He stops short at the sight of Blanche in the chair. She returns his look without flinching. Then he sits again at the poker table. Two of the men have started arguing hotly.*]

STEVE : I didn't hear you name it.

PABLO : Didn't I name it, Mitch?

MITCH : I wasn't listenin'.

PABLO : What were you doing, then?

STANLEY : He was looking through them drapes. [*He jumps up and jerks roughly at curtains to close them.*] Now deal the hand over again and let's play cards or quit. Some people get ants when they win.

[*Mitch rises as Stanley returns to his seat.*]

STANLEY : [*yelling*] Sit down!

MITCH : I'm going to the "head". Deal me out.

PABLO : Sure he's got ants now. Seven five-dollar bills in his pants pocket folded as tight as spitballs.

STEVE : Tomorrow you'll see him at the cashier's window getting them changed into quarters.

STANLEY : And when he goes home he'll deposit them one by one in a piggy bank his mother give him for Christmas. [*Dealing.*] This game is Spit in the Ocean.

[*Mitch laughs uncomfortably and continues through the portieres. He stops just inside.*]

BLANCHE : [*softly*] Hello! The Little Boys' Room is busy right now.

MITCH : We've—been drinking beer.

BLANCHE : I hate beer.

MITCH : It's—a hot weather drink.

BLANCHE : Oh, I don't think so; it always makes me warmer. Have you got any cigs? [*She has slipped on the dark red satin wrapper.*]

MITCH : Sure.

BLANCHE : What kind are they?

MITCH : Luckies.

BLANCHE : Oh, good. What a pretty case. Silver?

MITCH : Yes. Yes; read the inscription.

BLANCHE : Oh, is there an inscription? I can't make it out. [*He strikes a match and moves closer*] Oh! [*reading with feigned difficulty*]:
"And if God choose,
I shall but love thee better—after—death!" Why, that's from my favorite sonnet by Mrs. Browning!

MITCH : You know it?

BLANCHE : Certainly I do!

MITCH : There's a story connected with that inscription.

BLANCHE : It sounds like a romance.

MITCH : A pretty sad one.

BLANCHE : Oh?

MITCH : The girl's dead now.

BLANCHE : [*in a tone of deep sympathy*] Oh!

MITCH : She knew she was dying when she give me this. A very strange girl, very sweet—very!

BLANCHE : She must have been fond of you. Sick people have such deep, sincere attachments.

MITCH : That's right, they certainly do.

BLANCHE : Sorrow makes for sincerity, I think.

MITCH : It sure brings it out in people.

BLANCHE : The little there is belongs to people who have experienced some sorrow.

MITCH : I believe you are right about that.

BLANCHE : I'm positive that I am. Show me a person who hasn't known any sorrow and I'll show you a superficial— Listen to me! My tongue is a little-thick! You boys are responsible for it. The show let out at eleven and we couldn't come home on account of the poker game so we had to go somewhere and drink. I'm not accustomed to having more than one drink. Two is the limit—and *three!* [*She laughs*] Tonight I had three.

STANLEY : Mitch!

MITCH : Deal me out I'm talking to Miss—

BLANCHE : DuBois.

MITCH : Miss DuBois?

BLANCHE : It's a French name. It means woods and Blanche means white, so the two together mean white woods. Like an orchard in spring! You can remember it by that.

MITCH : You're French?

BLANCHE : We are French by extraction. Our first American ancestors were French Huguenots.

MITCH : You are Stella's sister, are you not?

BLANCHE : Yes, Stella is my precious little sister. I call her little in spite of the fact she's somewhat older than I. Just slightly. Less than a year. Will you do something for me?

MITCH : Sure. What?

BLANCHE : I bought this adorable little colored paper lantern at a Chinese shop on Bourbon. Put it over the light bulb! Will you, please?

MITCH : Be glad to.

BLANCHE : I can't stand a naked light bulb, any more than I can a rude remark or a vulgar action.

MITCH : [*adjusting the lantern*] I guess we strike you as being a pretty rough bunch.

BLANCHE : I'm very adaptable—to circumstances.

MITCH : Well, that's a good thing to be. You are visiting Stanley and Stella?

BLANCHE : Stella hasn't been so well lately, and I came down to help her for a while. She's very run down.

MITCH : You're not—?

BLANCHE : Married? No, no. I'm an old maid schoolteacher!

MITCH : You may teach school but you're certainly not an old maid.

BLANCHE : Thank you, sir! I appreciate your gallantry!

MITCH : So you are in the teaching profession?

BLANCHE : Yes. Ah, yes…

MITCH : Grade school or high school or—

STANLEY : [*bellowing*] Mitch!

MITCH : Coming!

BLANCHE : Gracious, what lung-power!... I teach high school. In Laurel.

MITCH : What do you teach? What subject?

BLANCHE : Guess!

MITCH : I bet you teach art or music? [*Blanche laughs delicately*] Of course I could be wrong. You might teach arithmetic.

BLANCHE : Never arithmetic, sir, never arithmetic! [*with a laugh*] I don't even know my multiplication tables! No, I have the misfortune of being an English instructor. I attempt to instill a bunch of bobby-soxers and drug-store Romeos with reverence for Hawthorne and Whitman and Poe!

MITCH : I guess that some of them are more interested in other things.

BLANCHE : How very right you are! Their literary heritage is not what most of them treasure above all else! But they're sweet things! And in the spring, it's touching to notice them making their first discovery of love! As if nobody had ever known it before!

[*The bathroom door opens and Stella comes out. Blanche continues talking to Mitch.*]

BLANCHE : Oh! Have you finished? Wait—I'll turn on the radio.

[She turns the knobs on the radio and it begins to play "Wien, Wien, nur du allein." Blanche waltzes to the music with romantic gestures. Mitch is delighted and moves in awkward imitation like a dancing bear.]

[Stanley stalks fiercely through the portieres into the bedroom. He crosses to the small white radio and snatches it off the table. With a shouted oath, he tosses the instrument out the window.]

STELLA : Drunk—drunk—animal thing, you! [*She rushes through to the poker table*] All of you—please go home! If any of you have one spark of decency in you—

BLANCHE : [*wildly*] Stella, watch out, he's—

[Stanley charges after Stella.]

MEN : [*feebly*] Take it easy, Stanley. Easy, fellow.—Let's all—

STELLA : You lay your hands on me and I'll—

[She backs out of sight. He advances and disappears. There is the sound of a blow. Stella cries out. Blanche screams and runs into the kitchen. The men rush forward and there is grappling and cursing. Something is overturned with a crash.]

BLANCHE : [*shrilly*] My sister is going to have a baby!

MITCH : This is terrible.

BLANCHE : Lunacy, absolute lunacy!

MITCH : Get him in here, men.

[Stanley is forced, pinioned by the two men, into the bedroom. He nearly throws them off. Then all at once he subsides and is limp in their grasp. They speak quietly and lovingly to him and he leans his face on one of their shoulders.]

STELLA : [*in a high, unnatural voice, out of sight*] I want to go away, I want to go away!

MITCH : Poker shouldn't be played in a house with women.

[*Blanche rushes into the bedroom.*]

BLANCHE : I want my sister's clothes! We'll go to that woman's upstairs!

MITCH : Where is the clothes?

BLANCHE : [*opening the closet*] I've got them! [*She rushes through to Stella*] Stella, Stella, precious! Dear, dear little sister, don't be afraid!

[*With her arms around Stella, Blanche guides her to the outside door and upstairs.*]

STANLEY : [*dully*] What's the matter; what's happened?

MITCH : You just blew your top, Stan.

PABLO : He's okay, now.

STEVE : Sure, my boy's okay!

MITCH : Put him on the bed and get a wet towel.

PABLO : I think coffee would do him a world of good, now.

STANLEY : [*thickly*] I want water.

MITCH : Put him under the shower!

[*The men talk quietly as they lead him to the bathroom.*]

STANLEY : Let go of me, you sons of bitches!

[*Sounds of blows are heard. The water goes on full tilt.*]

STEVE : Let's get quick out of here!

[*They rush to the poker table and sweep up their winnings on their way out.*]

MITCH : [*sadly but firmly*] Poker should not be played in a house with women.

[*The door closes on them and the place is still. The Negro entertainers in the bar around the corner play "Paper Doll" slow and blue. After a moment Stanley comes out of the bathroom dripping water and still in his clinging wet polka dot drawers.*]

STANLEY : Stella! [*There is a pause*] My baby doll's left me!

[*He breaks into sobs. Then he goes to the phone and dials, still shuddering with sobs.*]

Eunice? I want my baby. [*He waits a moment; then he hangs up and dials again*] Eunice! I'll keep on ringin' until I talk with my baby!

[*An indistinguishable shrill voice is heard. He hurls phone to floor. Dissonant brass and piano sounds as the rooms dim out to darkness and the outer walls appear in the night light. The "blue piano" plays for a brief interval.*]

[*Finally, Stanley stumbles half dressed out to the porch and down the wooden steps to the pavement before the building. There he throws back his head like a baying hound and bellows his wife's name: "Stella! Stella, sweetheart! Stella!"*]

STANLEY : Stellahhhhh!

EUNICE : [*calling down from the door of her upper apartment*] Quit that howling out there an' go back to bed!

STANLEY : I want my baby down here. Stella, Stella!

EUNICE : She ain't comin' down so you quit! Or you'll git th' law on you!

STANLEY : Stella!

EUNICE : You can't beat on a woman an' then call 'er back! She won't come! And her goin' t' have a baby!... You stinker! You whelp of a Polack, you! I hope they do haul you in and turn the fire hose on you, same as the last time!

STANLEY : [*humbly*] Eunice, I want my girl to come down with me!

EUNICE : Hah! [*She slams her door.*]

STANLEY : [*with heaven-splitting violence*] STELLLAHHHHH!

[*The low-tone clarinet moans. The door upstairs opens again. Stella slips down the rickety stairs in her robe. Her eyes are glistening with tears and her hair loose about her throat and shoulders. They stare at each other. Then they come together with low, animal moans. He falls to his knees on the steps and presses his face to her belly, curving a little with maternity. Her eyes go blind with tenderness as she catches his head and raises him level with her. He snatches the screen door open and lifts her off her feet and bears her into the dark flat.*]

[*Blanche comes out on the upper landing in her robe and slips fearfully down the steps.*]

BLANCHE : Where is my little sister? Stella? Stella?

[*She stops before the dark entrance of her sister's flat. Then catches her breath as if struck. She rushes down to the walk before the house. She looks right and left as if for a sanctuary.*]

[*The music fades away. Mitch appears from around the corner.*]

MITCH : Miss DuBois?

BLANCHE : Oh!

MITCH : All quiet on the Potomac now?

BLANCHE : She ran downstairs and went back in there with him.

MITCH : Sure she did.

BLANCHE : I'm terrified!

MITCH : Ho-ho! There's nothing to be scared of. They're crazy about each other.

BLANCHE : I'm not used to such—

MITCH : Naw, it's a shame this had to happen when you just got here. But don't take it serious.

BLANCHE : Violence! Is so—

MITCH : Set down on the steps and have a cigarette with me.

BLANCHE : I'm not properly dressed.

MITCH : That don't make no difference in the Quarter.

BLANCHE : Such a pretty silver case.

MITCH : I showed you the inscription, didn't I?

BLANCHE : Yes. [*During the pause, she looks up at the sky*] There's so much—so much confusion in the world... [*He coughs diffidently*] Thank you for being so kind! I need kindness now.

Scene 4

It is early the following morning. There is a confusion of street cries like a choral chant.

Stella is lying down in the bedroom. Her face is serene in the early morning sunlight. One hand rests on her belly, rounding slightly with new maternity. From the other dangles a book of colored comics. Her eyes and lips have that almost narcotized tranquility that is the faces of Eastern idols.

The table is sloppy with remains of breakfast and the debris of the preceding night, and Stanley's gaudy pyjamas lie across the threshold of the bathroom. The outside door is slightly ajar on a sky of summer brilliance.

Blanche appears at this door. She has spent a sleepless night and her appearance entirely contrasts with Stella's. She presses her knuckles nervously to her lips as she looks through the door, before entering.

BLANCHE : Stella?

STELLA : [*stirring lazily*] Hmmh?

[*Blanche utters a moaning cry and runs into the bedroom, throwing herself down beside Stella in a rush of hysterical tenderness.*]

BLANCHE : Baby, my baby sister!

STELLA : [*drawing away from her*] Blanche, what is the matter with you?

[*Blanche straightens up slowly and stands beside the bed looking down at her sister with knuckles pressed to her lips.*]

BLANCHE : He's left?

STELLA : Stan? Yes.

BLANCHE : Will he be back?

STELLA : He's gone to get the car greased. Why?

BLANCHE : Why! I've been half crazy, Stella! When I found out you'd been insane enough to come back in here after what happened—I started to rush in after you!

STELLA : I'm glad you didn't.

BLANCHE : What were you thinking of? [*Stella makes an indefinite gesture*] Answer me! What? What?

STELLA : Please, Blanche! Sit down and stop yelling.

BLANCHE : All right, Stella. I will repeat the question quietly now. How could you come back in this place last night? Why, you must have slept with him!

[*Stella gets up in a calm and leisurely way.*]

STELLA : Blanche, I'd forgotten how excitable you are. You're making much too much fuss about this.

BLANCHE : Am I?

STELLA : Yes, you are, Blanche. I know how it must have seemed to you and I'm awful sorry it had to happen, but it wasn't anything as serious as you seem to take it. In the first place, when men are drinking and playing poker anything can happen. It's always a powder-keg.

He didn't know what he was doing… He was as good as a lamb when I came back and he's really very, very ashamed of himself.

BLANCHE : And that—that makes it all right?

STELLA : No, it isn't all right for anybody to make such a terrible row, but—people do sometimes. Stanley's always smashed things. Why, on our wedding night—soon as we came in here—he snatched off one of my slippers and rushed about the place smashing the light bulbs with it.

BLANCHE : He did—what?

STELLA : He smashed all the light bulbs with the heel of my slipper! [*She laughs.*]

BLANCHE : And you—you *let* him? Didn't *run*, didn't *scream*?

STELLA : I was—sort of—thrilled by it. [*She waits for a moment.*] Eunice and you had breakfast?

BLANCHE : Do you suppose I wanted my breakfast?

STELLA : There's some coffee left on the stove.

BLANCHE : You're so—matter of fact about it, Stella.

STELLA : What other can I be? He's taken the radio to get it fixed. It didn't land on the pavement so only one tube was smashed.

BLANCHE : And you are standing there smiling!

STELLA : What do you want me to do?

BLANCHE : Pull yourself together and face the facts.

STELLA : What are they, in your opinion?

BLANCHE : In my opinion? You're married to a madman!

STELLA : No!

BLANCHE : Yes, you are, your fix is worse than mine is! Only you're not being sensible about it. I'm going to do something. Get hold of myself and make myself a new life!

STELLA : Yes?

BLANCHE : But you've given in. And that isn't right, you're not old! You can get out.

STELLA : [*slowly and emphatically*] I'm not in anything I want to get out of.

BLANCHE : [*incredulously*] What—Stella?

STELLA : I said I am not in anything that I have a desire to get out of. Look at the mess in this room! And those empty bottles! They went through two cases last night! He promised this morning that he was going to quit having these poker parties, but you know how long such a promise is going to keep. Oh, well, it's his pleasure, like mine is movies and bridge. People have got to tolerate each other's habits, I guess.

BLANCHE : I don't understand you. [*Stella turns toward her*] I don't understand your indifference. Is this a Chinese philosophy you've—cultivated?

STELLA : Is what—what?

BLANCHE : This—shuffling about and mumbling—"One tube smashed—beer bottles—mess in the kitchen."—as if nothing out of the ordinary has happened! [*Stella laughs uncertainly and picking up the broom, twirls it in her hands.*]

BLANCHE : Are you deliberately shaking that thing in my face?

STELLA : No.

BLANCHE : Stop it. Let go of that broom. I won't have you cleaning up for him!

STELLA : Then who's going to do it? Are you?

BLANCHE : I? I!

STELLA : No, I didn't think so.

BLANCHE : Oh, let me think, if only my mind would function! We've got to get hold of some money, that's the way out!

STELLA : I guess that money is always nice to get hold of.

BLANCHE : Listen to me. I have an idea of some kind. [*Shakily she twists a cigarette into her holder*] Do you remember Shep Huntleigh? [*Stella shakes her head.*] Of course you remember Shep Huntleigh. I went out with him at college and wore his pin for a while. Well—

STELLA : Well?

BLANCHE : I ran into him last winter. You know I went to Miami during the Christmas holidays?

STELLA : No.

BLANCHE : Well, I did. I took the trip as an investment, thinking I'd meet someone with a million dollars.

STELLA : Did you?

BLANCHE : Yes. I ran into Shep Huntleigh—I ran into him on Biscayne Boulevard, on Christmas Eve, about dusk... getting into his car—Cadillac convertible; must have been a block long!

STELLA : I should think it would have been—inconvenient in traffic!

BLANCHE : You've heard of oil-wells?

STELLA : Yes—remotely.

BLANCHE : He has them, all over Texas. Texas is literally spouting gold in his pockets.

STELLA : My, my.

BLANCHE : Y'know how indifferent I am to money. I think of money in terms of what it does for you. But he could do it, he could certainly do it!

STELLA : Do what, Blanche?

BLANCHE : Why—set us up in a—shop!

STELLA : What kind of a shop?

BLANCHE : Oh, a—shop of some kind! He could do it with half what his wife throws away at the races.

STELLA : He's married?

BLANCHE : Honey, would I be here if the man weren't married? [*Stella laughs a little. Blanche suddenly springs up and crosses to phone. She speaks shrilly*] How do I get Western Union?—Operator! Western Union!

STELLA : That's a dial phone, honey.

BLANCHE : can't dial, I'm too—

STELLA : Just dial O.

BLANCHE : O?

STELLA : Yes, "O" for Operator! [*Blanche considers a moment; then she puts the phone down.*]

BLANCHE : Give me a pencil. Where is a slip of paper? I've got to write it down first—the message, I mean…

[*She goes to the dressing table, and grabs up a sheet of Kleenex and an eyebrow pencil for writing equipment.*]

Let me see now… [*She bites the pencil*] "Darling Shep. Sister and I in desperate situation."

STELLA : I beg your pardon!

BLANCHE : "Sister and I in desperate situation. Will explain details later. Would you be interested in—?" [*She bites the pencil again*] "Would you be—interested—in…" [*She smashes the pencil on the table and springs up*] You never get anywhere with direct appeals!

STELLA : [*with a laugh*] Don't be so ridiculous, darling!

BLANCHE : But I'll think of something, I've got to think of—something! Don't, don't laugh at me, Stella! Please, please don't—I—I want you to look at the contents of my purse! Here's what's in it! [*She snatches her purse open*] Sixty-five measly cents in coin of the realm!

STELLA : [*crossing to bureau*] Stanley doesn't give me a regular allowance, he likes to pay bills himself, but—this morning he gave me ten dollars to smooth things over. You take five of it, Blanche, and I'll keep the rest

BLANCHE : Oh, no. No, Stella.

STELLA : [*insisting*] I know how it helps your morale just having a little pocket-money on you.

BLANCHE : No, thank you—I'll take to the streets!

STELLA : Talk sense! How did you happen to get so low on funds?

BLANCHE : Money just goes—it goes places. [*She rubs her forehead*] Sometime today I've got to get hold of a bromo!

STELLA : I'll fix you one now.

BLANCHE : Not yet—I've got to keep thinking!

STELLA : I wish you'd just let things go, at least for a—while...

BLANCHE : Stella, I can't live with him! You can, he's your husband. But how could I stay here with him, after last night, with, just those curtains between us?

STELLA : Blanche, you saw him at his worst last night.

BLANCHE : On the contrary, I saw him at his best! What such a man has to offer is animal force and he gave a wonderful exhibition of that! But the only way to live with such a man is to—go to bed with him! And that's your job—not mine!

STELLA : After you've rested a little, you'll see it's going to work out. You don't have to worry about anything while you're here. I mean—expenses...

BLANCHE : I have to plan for us both, to get us both—out!

STELLA : You take it for granted that I am in something that I want to get out of.

BLANCHE : I take it for granted that you still have sufficient memory of Belle Reve to find this place and these poker players impossible to live with.

STELLA : Well, you're taking entirely too much for granted.

BLANCHE : I can't believe you're in earnest.

STELLA : No?

BLANCHE : I understand how it happened—a little. You saw him in uniform, an officer, not here but—

STELLA : I'm not sure it would have made any difference where I saw him.

BLANCHE : Now don't say it was one of those mysterious electric things between people! If you do I'll laugh in your face.

STELLA : I am not going to say anything more at all about it!

BLANCHE : All right, then, don't!

STELLA : But there are things that happen between a man and a woman in the dark—that sort of make everything else seem—unimportant [*Pause.*]

BLANCHE : What you are talking about is brutal desire—just—Desire!—the name of that rattle-trap streetcar that bangs through the Quarter, up one old narrow street and down another…

STELLA : Haven't you ever ridden on that streetcar?

BLANCHE : It brought me here.—Where I'm not wanted and where I'm ashamed to be…

STELLA : Then don't you think your superior attitude is a bit out of place?

BLANCHE : I am not being or feeling at all superior, Stella. Believe me I'm not! It's just this. This is how I look at it. A man like that is someone to go out with—once—twice—three times when the devil is in you. But live with? Have a child by?

STELLA : I have told you I love him.

BLANCHE : Then I tremble for you! I just—tremble for you...

STELLA : I can't help your trembling if you insist on trembling! [*There is a pause.*]

BLANCHE : May I—speak—plainly?

STELLA : Yes, do. Go ahead. As plainly as you want to.

[*Outside, a train approaches. They are silent till the noise subsides. They are both in the bedroom.*]

[*Under cover of the train's noise Stanley enters from outside. He stands unseen by the women, holding some packages in his arms, and overhears their following conversation. He wears an undershirt and grease-stained seersucker pants.*]

BLANCHE : Well—if you'll forgive me—he's common!

STELLA : Why, yes, I suppose he is.

BLANCHE : Suppose! You can't have forgotten that much of our bringing up, Stella, that you just suppose that any part of a gentleman's in his nature! Not one particle, no! Oh, if he was just—ordinary! Just plain—but good and wholesome, but—no. There's something downright—bestial—about him! You're hating me saying this, aren't you?

STELLA : [*coldly*] Go on and say it all, Blanche.

BLANCHE : He acts like an animal, has an animal's habits! Eats like one, moves like one, talks like one! There's even something—sub-human—something not quite to the stage of humanity yet! Yes, something—ape-like about him, like one of those pictures I've seen in—anthropological studies! Thousands and thousands of years have passed him right by, and there he is—Stanley Kowalski— survivor of the stone age! Bearing the raw meat home from the kill in the jungle! And you—

you here—*waiting* for him! Maybe he'll strike you or maybe grunt and kiss you! That is, if kisses have been discovered yet! Night falls and the other apes gather! There in the front of the cave, all grunting like him, and swilling and gnawing and hulking! His poker night!—you call it—this party of apes! Somebody growls—some creature snatches at something—the fight is on! *God*! Maybe we are a long way from being made in God's image, but Stella—my sister—there has been *some* progress since then! Such things as art—as poetry and music—such kinds of new light have come into the world since then! In some kinds of people some tenderer feelings have had some little beginning! That we have got to make *grow*! And *cling* to, and hold as our flag! In this dark march toward whatever it is we're approaching... *Don't—don't hang back with the brutes!*

[*Another train passes outside. Stanley hesitates, licking his lips. Then suddenly he turns stealthily about and withdraws through front door. The women are still unaware of his presence. When the train has passed he calls through the closed front door.*]

STANLEY : Hey! Hey, Stella!

STELLA : [*who has listened gravely to Blanche*] Stanley!

BLANCHE : Stell, I

[*But Stella has gone to the front door. Stanley enters casually with his packages.*]

STANLEY : Hiyuh, Stella. Blanche back?

STELLA : Yes, she's back.

STANLEY : Hiyuh, Blanche. [*He grins at her.*]

STELLA : You must've got under the car.

STANLEY : Them dam mechanics at Fritz's don't know their ass fr'm—Hey!

[*Stella has embraced him—with both arms, fiercely, and full in the view of Blanche. He laughs and clasps her head to him. Over her head he grins through the curtains at Blanche.*]

[*As the lights fade away, with a lingering brightness on their embrace, the music of the "blue piano" and trumpet and drums is heard.*]

Scene 5

Blanche is seated in the bedroom fanning herself with a palm leaf as she reads over a just completed letter. Suddenly she bursts into a peal of laughter. Stella is dressing in the bedroom.

STELLA : What are you laughing at, honey?

BLANCHE : Myself, myself, for being such a liar! I'm writing a letter to Shep. [*She picks up the letter*] "Darling Shep. I am spending the summer on the wing, making flying visits here and there. And who knows, perhaps I shall take a sudden notion to swoop down on Dallas! How would you feel about that? Ha-ha! [*She laughs nervously and brightly, touching her throat as if actually talking to Shep*] Forewarned is forearmed, as they say!"—How does that sound?

STELLA : Uh-huh...

BLANCHE : [*going on nervously*] "Most of my sister's friends go north in the summer but some have homes on the Gulf and there has been a continued round of entertainments, teas, cocktails, and luncheons—"

[*A disturbance is heard upstairs at the Hubbells' apartment.*]

STELLA : Eunice seems to be having some trouble with Steve.

[*Eunice's voice shouts in terrible wrath.*]

EUNICE : I heard about you and that blonde!

STEVE : That's a damn lie!

EUNICE : You ain't pulling the wool over my eyes! I wouldn't mind if you'd stay down at the Four Deuces, but you always going up.

STEVE : Who ever seen me up?

EUNICE : I seen you chasing her 'round the balcony—I'm gonna call the vice squad!

STEVE : Don't you throw that at me!

EUNICE : [*shrieking*] You hit me! I'm gonna call the police!

[*A clatter of aluminum striking a wall is heard, followed by a man's angry roar, shouts and overturned furniture. There is a crash; then a relative hush.*]

BLANCHE : [*brightly*] Did he *kill* her?

[*Eunice appears on the steps in daemonic disorder.*]

STELLA : No! She's coming downstairs.

EUNICE : Call the police. I'm going to call the police! [*She rushes around the comer.*]

[*They laugh lightly. Stanley comes around the corner in his green-and-scarlet silk bowling shirt. He trots up the steps and bangs into the kitchen. Blanche registers his entrance with nervous gestures.*]

STANLEY : What's a matter with Eun-uss?

STELLA : She and Steve had a row. Has she got the police?

STANLEY : Naw. She's gettin' a drink.

STELLA : That's much more practical!

[*Steve comes down nursing a bruise on his forehead and looks in the door.*]

STEVE : She here?

STANLEY : Naw, naw. At the Four Deuces.

STEVE : That rutting hunk! [*He looks around the corner a bit timidly, then turns with affected boldness and runs after her.*]

BLANCHE : I must jot that down in my notebook. Ha-ha! I'm compiling a notebook of quaint little words and phrases I've picked up here.

STANLEY : You won't pick up nothing here you ain't heard before.

BLANCHE : Can I count on that?

STANLEY : You can count on it up to five hundred.

BLANCHE : That's a mighty high number. [*He jerks open the bureau drawer, slams it shut and throws shoes in a corner. At each noise Blanche winces slightly. Finally she speaks*] What sign were you born under?

STANLEY : [*while he is dressing*] Sign?

BLANCHE : Astrological sign. I bet you were born under Aries. Aries people are forceful and dynamic. They dote on noise! They love to bang things around! You must have had lots of banging around in the army and now that you're out, you make up for it by treating inanimate objects with such a fury!

[*Stella has been going in and out of closet during this scene. Now she pops her head out of the closet.*]

STELLA : Stanley was born just five minutes after Christmas.

BLANCHE : Capricorn—the Goat!

STANLEY : What sign were you born under?

BLANCHE : Oh, my birthday's next month, the fifteenth of September; that's under Virgo.

STANLEY : What's Virgo?

BLANCHE : Virgo is the Virgin.

STANLEY : [*contemptuously*] Bah! [*He advances a little as he knots his tie*] Say, do you happen to know somebody named Shaw?

[*Her face expresses a faint shock. She reaches for the cologne bottle and dampens her handkerchief as she answers carefully.*]

BLANCHE : Why, everybody knows somebody named Shaw!

STANLEY : Well, this somebody named Shaw is under the impression he met you in Laurel, but I figure he must have got you mixed up with some other party because this other party is someone he met at a hotel called the Flamingo.

[*Blanche laughs breathlessly as she touches the cologne-dampened handkerchief to her temples.*]

BLANCHE : I'm afraid he does have me mixed up with this "other party." The Hotel Flamingo is not the sort of establishment I would dare to be seen in!

STANLEY : You know of it?

BLANCHE : Yes, I've seen it and smelled it.

STANLEY : You must've got pretty close if you could smell it.

BLANCHE : The odor of cheap perfume is penetrating.

STANLEY : That stuff you use is expensive?

BLANCHE : Twenty-five dollars an ounce! I'm nearly out. That's just a hint if you want to remember my birthday! [*She speaks lightly but her voice has a note of fear.*]

STANLEY : Shaw must've got you mixed up. He goes in and out of Laurel all the time so he can check on it and clear up any mistake.

[*He turns away and crosses to the portieres. Blanche closes her eyes as if faint. Her hand trembles as she lifts the handkerchief again to her forehead.*]

[*Steve and Eunice come around corner. Steve's arm is around Eunice's shoulder and she is sobbing luxuriously and he is cooing love-words. There is a murmur of thunder as they go slowly upstairs in a tight embrace.*]

STANLEY : [*to Stella*] I'll wait for you at the Four Deuces!

STELLA : Hey! Don't I rate one kiss?

STANLEY : Not in front of your sister.

[*He goes out. Blanche rises from her chair. She seems faint; looks about her with an expression of almost panic.*]

BLANCHE : Stella! What have you heard about me?

STELLA : Huh?

BLANCHE : What have people been telling you about me?

STELLA : Telling?

BLANCHE : You haven't heard any—unkind—gossip about me?

STELLA : Why, no, Blanche, of course not!

BLANCHE : Honey, there was—a good deal of talk in Laurel.

STELLA : About you, Blanche?

BLANCHE : I wasn't so good the last two years or so, after Belle Reve had started to slip through my fingers.

STELLA : All of us do things we—

BLANCHE : I never was hard or sell-sufficient enough. When people are soft—soft people have got to shimmer and glow—they've got to put on soft colors, the colors of butterfly wings, and put a— paper lantern over the light… It isn't enough to be soft. You've got to be soft and attractive. And I—I'm fading now! I don't know how much longer I can turn the trick.

[*The afternoon has faded to dusk. Stella goes into the bedroom and turns on the light under the paper lantern. She holds a bottled soft drink in her hand.*]

BLANCHE : Have you been listening to me?

STELLA : I don't listen to you when you are being morbid! [*She advances with the bottled coke.*]

BLANCHE : [*with abrupt change to gaiety*] Is that coke for me?

STELLA : Not for anyone else!

BLANCHE : Why, you precious thing, you! Is it just coke?

STELLA : [*turning*] You mean you want a shot in it!

BLANCHE : Well, honey, a shot never does a coke any harm! Let me! You mustn't wait on me!

STELLA : I like to wait on you, Blanche. It makes it seem more like home. [*She goes into the kitchen, finds a glass and pours a shot of whiskey into it.*]

BLANCHE : I have to admit I love to be waited on…

[*She rushes into the bedroom. Stella goes to her with the glass. Blanche suddenly clutches Stella's free hand with a moaning sound and presses the hand to her lips. Stella is embarrassed by her show of emotion. Blanche speaks in a choked voice.*]

You're—you're—so good to me! And I—

STELLA : Blanche.

BLANCHE : I know, I won't! You hate me to talk sentimental! But honey, believe I feel things more than I tell you! I won't stay long! I won't, I promise I—

STELLA : Blanche!

BLANCHE : [*hysterically*] I won't, I promise, I'll go! Go soon! I will really! I won't hang around until he—throws me out…

STELLA : Now will you stop talking foolish?

BLANCHE : Yes, honey. Watch how you pour—that fizzy stuff foams over!

[*Blanche laughs shrilly and grabs the glass, but her handshakes so it almost slips from her grasp. Stella pours the coke into the glass. It foams over and spills. Blanche gives a piercing cry.*]

STELLA : [*shocked by the cry*] Heavens!

BLANCHE : Right on my pretty white skirt!

STELLA : Oh… Use my hanky. Blot gently.

BLANCHE : [*slowly recovering*] know—gently—gently…

STELLA : Did it stain?

BLANCHE : Not a bit. Ha-ha! Isn't that lucky? [*She sits down shaking, taking a grateful drink. She holds the glass in both hands and continues to laugh a little.*]

STELLA : Why did you scream like that?

BLANCHE : I don't know why I screamed! [*continuing nervously*] Mitch—Mitch is coming at seven. I guess I am just feeling nervous about our relations. [*She begins to talk rapidly and breathlessly*] He hasn't gotten a thing but a goodnight kiss, that's all I have given him, Stella. I want his respect. And men don't want anything they get too easy. But on the other hand men lose interest quickly. Especially when the girl is over—thirty. They think a girl over thirty ought to—the vulgar term is—"put out."… And I—I'm not "putting out." Of course he—he doesn't know—I mean I haven't informed him—of my real age!

STELLA : Why are you sensitive about your age?

BLANCHE : Because of hard knocks my vanity's been given. What I mean is—he thinks I'm sort of—prim and proper, you know! [*She laughs out sharply*] I want to deceive him enough to make him—want me…

STELLA : Blanche, do you want him?

BLANCHE : I want to rest! I want to breathe quietly again! Yes—I want Mitch... *very badly*! Just think! If it happens, I can leave here and not be anyone's problem…

[*Stanley comes around the corner with a drink under his belt.*]

STANLEY : [*bawling*] Hey, Steve! Hey, Eunice! Hey, Stella!

[*There are joyous calls from above. Trumpet and drums are heard from around the corner.*]

STELLA : [*kissing Blanche impulsively*] It will happen!

BLANCHE : [*doubtfully*] It will?

STELLA : It will! [*She goes across into the kitchen, looking back at Blanche.*] It will, honey, it will… But don't take another drink! [*Her voice catches as she goes out the door to meet her husband.*]

[*Blanche sinks faintly back in her chair—with her drink. Eunice shrieks with laughter and runs down the steps. Steve bounds after her—with goat-like screeches and chases her around corner. Stanley and Stella twine arms as they follow, laughing.*]

[*Dusk settles deeper. The music from the Four Deuces is slow and blue.*]

BLANCHE : Ah, me, ah, me, ah, me…

[*Her eyes fall shut and the palm leaf fan drops from her fingers. She slaps her hand on the chair arm a couple of times. There is a little glimmer of lightning about the building.*]

[*A Young Man comes along the street and rings the bell.*]

BLANCHE : Come in.

[*The Young Man appears through the portieres. She regards him with interest.*]

BLANCHE : Well, well! What can I do for you?

YOUNG MAN: I'm collecting for The Evening Star.

BLANCHE : I didn't know that stars took up collections.

YOUNG MAN: It's the paper.

BLANCHE : I know. I was joking—feebly! Will you—have a drink?

YOUNG MAN: No, ma'am. No, thank you. I can't drink on the job.

BLANCHE : Oh, well, now, let's see... No, I don't have a dime! I'm not the lady of the house. I'm her sister from Mississippi. I'm one of those poor relations you've heard about.

YOUNG MAN: That's all right I'll drop by later. [*He starts to go out. She approaches a little.*]

BLANCHE : Hey! [*He turns back shyly. She puts a cigarette in a long holder*] Could you give me a light? [*She crosses toward him. They meet at the door between the two rooms.*]

YOUNG MAN: Sure. [*He takes out a lighter*] This doesn't always work.

BLANCHE : It's temperamental? [*It flares*] Ah!—thank you. [*He starts away again*] Hey! [*He turns again, still more uncertainly. She goes close to him*] Uh—what time is it?

YOUNG MAN: Fifteen of seven, ma'am.

BLANCHE : So late? Don't you just love these long rainy afternoons in New Orleans when an hour isn't just an hour—but a little piece of eternity dropped into your hands—and who knows what to do with it? [*She touches his shoulders.*] You—uh—didn't get wet in the rain?

YOUNG MAN: No, ma'am. I stepped inside.

BLANCHE : In a drug-store? And had a soda?

YOUNG MAN: Uh-huh.

BLANCHE : Chocolate?

YOUNG MAN: No, ma'am. Cherry.

BLANCHE : [*laughing*] Cherry!

YOUNG MAN: A cherry soda.

BLANCHE : You make my mouth water. [*She touches his cheek lightly, and smiles. Then she goes to the trunk.*]

YOUNG MAN: Well, I'd better be going—

BLANCHE : [*stopping him*] Young man!

[He turns. She takes a large, gossamer scarf from the trunk and drapes it about her shoulders.]

[In the ensuing pause, the "blue piano" is heard. It continues through the rest of this scene and the opening of the next. The young man clears his throat and looks yearningly at the door.]

Young man! Young, young, young man! Has anyone ever told you that you look like a young Prince out of the Arabian Nights?

[The Young Man laughs uncomfortably and stands like a bashful kid. Blanche speaks softly to him.]

Well, you do, honey lamb! Come here. I want to kiss you, just once, softly and sweetly on your mouth!

[Without waiting for him to accept, she crosses quickly to him and presses her lips to his.]

Now run along, now, quickly! It would be nice to keep you, but I've got to be good—and keep my hands off children.

[He stares at her a moment. She opens the door for him and blows a kiss at him as he goes down the steps with a dazed look. She stands there a little dreamily after he has disappeared. Then Mitch appears around the corner with a bunch of roses.]

BLANCHE : [*gaily*] Look who's coming! My Rosenkavalier! Bow to me first... now present them! Ahhh—Merciiii!

[She looks at him over them, coquettishly pressing them to her lips. He beams at her self-consciously.]

Scene 6

It is about two A.M. on the same evening. The outer wall of the building is visible. Blanche and Mitch come in. The utter exhaustion which only a neurasthenic personality can know is evident in Blanche's voice and manner. Mitch is stolid but depressed. They have probably been out to the amusement park on Lake Pontchartrain, for Mitch is bearing, upside down, a plaster statuette of Mae West, the sort of prize won at shooting-galleries and carnival games of chance.

BLANCHE : [*stopping lifelessly at the steps*] Well—
[*Mitch laughs uneasily.*]
Well...

MITCH : I guess it must be pretty late—and you're tired.

BLANCHE : Even the hot tamale man has deserted the street, and he hangs on till the end. [*Mitch laughs uneasily again*] How will you get home?

MITCH : I'll walk over to Bourbon and catch an owl-car.

BLANCHE : [*laughing grimly*] Is that streetcar named Desire still grinding along the tracks at this hour?

MITCH : [*heavily*] I'm afraid you haven't gotten much fun out of this evening, Blanche.

BLANCHE : I spoiled it for you.

MITCH : No, you didn't, but I felt all the time that I wasn't giving you much—entertainment.

BLANCHE : I simply couldn't rise to the occasion. That was all. I don't think I've ever tried so hard to be gay and made such a dismal mess of it. I get ten points for trying!—I did try.

MITCH : Why did you try if you didn't feel like it, Blanche?

BLANCHE : I was just obeying the law of nature.

MITCH : Which law is that?

BLANCHE : The one that says the lady must entertain the gentleman—or no dice! See if you can locate my door-key in this purse. When I'm so tired my fingers are all thumbs!

MITCH : [*rooting in her purse*] This it?

BLANCHE : No, honey, that's the key to my trunk which I must soon be packing.

MITCH : You mean you are leaving here soon?

BLANCHE : I've outstayed my welcome.

MITCH : This it?

[*The music fades away.*]

BLANCHE : Eureka! Honey, you open the door while I take a last look at the sky. [*She leans on the porch rail. He opens the door and stands awkwardly behind her.*] I'm looking for the Pleiades, the Seven Sisters, but these girls are not out tonight. Oh, yes they are, there they are! God bless them! All in a bunch going home from their little bridge party... Y'get the door open? Good boy! I guess you—want to go now...

[*He shuffles and coughs a little.*]

MITCH : Can I—uh—kiss you-goodnight?

BLANCHE : Why do you always ask me if you may?

MITCH : I don't know whether you want me to or not.

BLANCHE : Why should you be so doubtful?

MITCH : That night when we parked by the lake and I kissed you, you—

BLANCHE : Honey, it wasn't the kiss I objected to. I liked the kiss very much. It was the other little— familiarity— that I—felt obliged to—discourage… I didn't resent it! Not a bit in the world! In fact, I was somewhat flattered that you—desired me! But, honey, you know as well as I do that a single girl, a girl alone in the world, has got to keep a firm hold on her emotions or she'll be lost!

MITCH : [*solemnly*] Lost?

BLANCHE : I guess you are used to girls that like to be lost. The kind that get lost immediately, on the first date!

MITCH : I like you to be exactly the way that you are, because in all my—experience—I have never known anyone like you. [*Blanche looks at him gravely; then she bursts into laughter and then claps a hand to her mouth.*]

MITCH : Are you laughing at me?

BLANCHE : No, honey. The lord and lady of the house have not yet returned, so come in. We'll have a night-cap. Let's leave the lights off. Shall we?

MITCH : You just—do what you want to.

[*Blanche precedes him into the kitchen. The outer wall of the building disappears and the interiors of the two rooms can be dimly seen.*]

BLANCHE : [*remaining in the first room*] The other room's more comfortable—go on in. This crashing around in the dark is my search for some liquor.

MITCH : You want a drink?

BLANCHE : I want you to have a drink! You have been so anxious and solemn all evening, and so have I; we have both been anxious and solemn and now for these few last remaining moments of our lives together—I want to create—joie de vivre! I'm lighting a candle.

MITCH : That's good.

BLANCHE : We are going to be very Bohemian. We are going to pretend that we are sitting in a little artists' cafe on the Left Bank in Paris! [*She lights a candle stub and puts it in a bottle.*] Le suis la Dame aux Camellias! Vous etes—Armand! Understand French?

MITCH : [*heavily*] Naw. Naw. I—

BLANCHE : Voutez-vous coucher avec moi ce soir? Vous ne comprenez pas? Ah, auelle dommage!—I mean it's a damned good thing... I've found some liquor. Just enough for two shots without any dividends, honey...

MITCH : [*heavily*] That's—good.

[*She enters the bedroom with the drinks and the candle*]

BLANCHE : Sit down! Why don't you take off your coat and loosen your collar?

MITCH : I better leave it on.

BLANCHE : No. I want you to be comfortable.

MITCH : I am ashamed of the way I perspire. My shirt is sticking to me.

BLANCHE : Perspiration is healthy. If people didn't perspire they would die in five minutes. [*She takes his coat from him*] This is a nice coat. What kind of material is it?

MITCH : They call that stuff alpaca.

BLANCHE : Oh. Alpaca.

MITCH : It's very light weight alpaca.

BLANCHE : Oh. Light weight alpaca.

MITCH : I don't like to wear a wash-coat even in summer because I sweat through it.

BLANCHE : Oh.

MITCH : And it don't look neat on me. A man with a heavy build has got to be careful of what he puts on him so he don't look too clumsy.

BLANCHE : You are not too heavy.

MITCH : You don't think I am?

BLANCHE : You are not the delicate type. You have a massive bone-structure and a very imposing physique.

MITCH : Thank you. Last Christmas I was given a membership to the New Orleans Athletic Club.

BLANCHE : Oh, good.

MITCH : It was the finest present I ever was given. I work out there with the weights and I swim and keep myself fit. When I started there, I was getting soft in the belly but now my belly is hard. It is so hard now that a man can punch me in the belly and it don't hurt me. Punch me! Go on! See? [*She pokes lightly at him.*]

BLANCHE : Gracious. [*Her hand touches her chest.*]

MITCH : Guess how much I weigh, Blanche?

BLANCHE : Oh, I'd say in the vicinity of—one hundred and eighty?

MITCH : Guess again.

BLANCHE : Not that much?

MITCH : No. More.

BLANCHE : Well, you're a tall man and you can carry a good deal of weight without looking awkward.

MITCH : I weigh two hundred and seven pounds and I'm six feet one and one-half inches tall in my bare feet—without shoes on. And that is what I weigh stripped.

BLANCHE : Oh, my goodness, me! It's awe-inspiring.

MITCH : [*embarrassed*] My weight is not a very interesting subject to talk about.

[*He hesitates for a moment*] What's yours?

BLANCHE : My weight?

MITCH : Yes.

BLANCHE : Guess!

MITCH : Let me lift you.

BLANCHE : Samson! Go on, lift me. [*He comes behind her and puts his hands on her waist and raises her lightly off the ground*] Well?

MITCH : You are light as a feather.

BLANCHE : Ha-ha! [*He lowers her but keeps his hands on her waist. Blanche speaks with an affectation of demureness*] You may release me now.

MITCH : Huh?

BLANCHE : [*giddly*] I said unhand me, sir. [*He fumblingly embraces her. Her voice sounds gently reproving*] Now, Mitch. Just because Stanley and Stella aren't at home is no reason why you shouldn't behave like a gentleman.

MITCH : Just give me a slap whenever I step out of bounds.

BLANCHE : That won't be necessary. You're a natural gentleman, one of the very few that are left in the world. I don't want you to think that I am severe and old maid school teacherish or anything like that. It's just—well—

MITCH : Huh?

BLANCHE : I guess it is just that I have—old-fashioned ideals! [*She rolls her eyes, knowing he cannot see her face. Mitch goes to the front door. There is a considerable silence between them. Blanche sighs and Mitch coughs self-consciously.*]

MITCH : [*finally*] Where's Stanley and Stella tonight?

BLANCHE : They have gone out With Mr. and Mrs. Hubbell upstairs.

MITCH : Where did they go?

BLANCHE : I think they were planning to go to a midnight prevue at Loew's State.

MITCH : We should all go out together some night.

BLANCHE : No. That wouldn't be a good plan.

MITCH : Why not?

BLANCHE : You are an old friend of Stanley's?

MITCH : We was together in the Two-forty-first.

BLANCHE : I guess he talks to you frankly?

MITCH : Sure.

BLANCHE : Has he talked to you about me?

MITCH : Oh—not very much.

BLANCHE : The way you say that, I suspect that he has.

MITCH : No, he hasn't said much.

BLANCHE : But what he *has* said. What would you say his attitude toward me was?

MITCH : Why do you want to ask that?

BLANCHE : Well—

MITCH : Don't you get along with him?

BLANCHE : What do you think?

MITCH : I don't think he understands you.

BLANCHE : That is putting it mildly. If it weren't for Stella about to have a baby, I wouldn't be able to endure things here.

MITCH : He isn't—nice to you?

BLANCHE : He is insufferably rude. Goes out of his way to offend me.

MITCH : In what way, Blanche?

BLANCHE : Why, in every conceivable way.

MITCH : I'm surprised to hear that.

BLANCHE : Are you?

MITCH : Well, I—don't see how anybody could be rude to you.

BLANCHE : It's really a pretty frightful situation. You see, there's no privacy here. There's just these portieres between the two rooms at night. He stalks through the rooms in his underwear at night. And I have to ask him to close the bathroom door. That sort of commonness isn't necessary. You probably wonder why I don't move out. Well, I'll tell you frankly. A teacher's salary is barely sufficient for her living expenses. I didn't save a penny last year and so I had to come here for the summer. That's why I have to put up with my sister's husband. And he has to put up with me, apparently so much against his wishes... Surely he must have told you how much he hates me!

MITCH : I don't think he hates you.

BLANCHE : He hates me. Or why would he insult me? The first time I laid eyes on him I thought to myself, that man is my executioner! That man will destroy me, unless—

MITCH : Blanche—

BLANCHE : Yes, honey?

MITCH : Can I ask you a question?

BLANCHE : Yes. What?

MITCH : How old are you?

[*She makes a nervous gesture.*]

BLANCHE : Why do you want to know?

MITCH : I talked to my mother about you and she said, "How old is Blanche?" And I wasn't able to tell her. [*There is another pause.*]

BLANCHE : You talked to your mother about me?

MITCH : Yes.

BLANCHE : Why?

MITCH : I told my mother how nice you were, and I liked you.

BLANCHE : Were you sincere about that?

MITCH : You know I was.

BLANCHE : Why did your mother want to know my age?

MITCH : Mother is sick.

BLANCHE : I'm sorry to hear it. Badly?

MITCH : She won't live long. Maybe just a few months.

BLANCHE : Oh.

MITCH : She worries because I'm not settled.

BLANCHE : Oh.

MITCH : She wants me to be settled down before she—[*His voice is hoarse and he clears his throat twice, shuffling nervously around with his hands in and out of his pockets.*]

BLANCHE : You love her very much, don't you?

MITCH : Yes.

BLANCHE : I think you have a great capacity for devotion. You will be lonely when she passes on, won't you? [*Mitch clears his throat and nods.*] I understand what that is.

MITCH : To be lonely?

BLANCHE : I loved someone, too, and the person I loved I lost.

MITCH : Dead? [*She crosses to the window and sits on the sill, looking out. She pours herself another drink.*] A man?

BLANCHE : He was a boy, just a boy, when I was a very young girl. When I was sixteen, I made the discovery—love. All at once and much, much too completely. It was like you suddenly turned a blinding light on something that had always been half in shadow, that's how it struck the world for me. But I was unlucky. Deluded. There was something different about the boy, a nervousness, a softness and tenderness which wasn't like a man's, although he wasn't the least bit effeminate looking—still—that thing was there... He came to me for help. I didn't know that. I didn't find out anything till after our marriage when we'd run away and come back and all I knew was I'd failed him in some mysterious way and wasn't able to give the help he needed but couldn't speak of! He was in the quick sands and clutching at me—but I wasn't holding him out, I was slipping in with him! I didn't know that. I didn't know anything except I loved him unendurably but without being able to help him or help myself. Then I found out. In the worst of all possible ways. By coming suddenly into a room that I thought was empty—which wasn't empty, but had two people in it... the boy I had married and an older man who had been his friend for years...

[*A locomotive is heard approaching outside. She claps her hands to her ears and crouches over. The headlight of the locomotive glares into the room as it thunders past. As the noise recedes she straightens slowly and continues speaking.*]

Afterwards we pretended that nothing had been discovered. Yes, the three of us drove out to Moon Lake Casino, very drunk and laughing all the way.

[*Polka music sounds. In a minor key faint with distance.*]

We danced the Varsouviana! Suddenly in the middle of the dance the boy I had married broke away from me and ran out of the casino. A few moments later—a shot!

[*The polka stops abruptly.*]

[*Blanche rises stiffly. Then, the polka resumes in a major key.*]

I ran out—all did!—all ran and gathered about the terrible thing at the edge of the lake! I couldn't get near for the crowding. Then somebody caught my arm.

"Don't go any closer! Come back! You don't want to see!" See? See what! Then I heard voices say Allan! Allan! The Grey boy! He'd stuck the revolver into his mouth, and fired—so that the back of his head had been—blown away!

[*She sways and covers her face.*]

It was because—on the dance-floor—unable to stop myself—I'd suddenly said—"I saw! I know! You disgust me..." And then the searchlight which had been turned on the world was turned off again and never for one moment since has there been any light that's stronger than this—kitchen— candle…

[*Mitch gets up awkwardly and moves toward her a little. The polka music increases. Mitch stands beside her.*]

MITCH : [*drawing her slowly into his arms*] You need somebody. And I need somebody too. Could it be—you and me, Blanche?

[*She stares at him vacantly for a moment. Then with a soft cry huddles in his embrace. She makes a sobbing effort to speak but the words won't come. He kisses her forehead and her eyes and finally her lips. The polka tune fades out. Her breath is drawn and released in long, grateful sobs.*]

BLANCHE : Sometimes—there's God—so quickly!

Scene 7

It is late afternoon in mid-September. The portieres are open and a table is set for a birthday supper, with cake and flowers. Stella is completing the decorations as Stanley comes in.

STANLEY : What's all this stuff for?

STELLA : Honey, it's Blanche's birthday.

STANLEY : She here?

STELLA : In the bathroom.

STANLEY : [*mimicking*] "Washing out some things"?

STELLA : I reckon so.

STANLEY : How long she been in there?

STELLA : All afternoon.

STANLEY : [*mimicking*] "Soaking in a hot tub"?

STELLA : Yes.

STANLEY : Temperature 100 on the nose, and she soaks herself in a hot tub.

STELLA : She says it cools her off for the evening.

STANLEY : And you run out an' get her cokes, I suppose? And serve 'em to Her Majesty in the tub? [*Stella shrugs*] Set down here a minute.

STELLA : Stanley, I've got things to do.

STANLEY : Set down! I've got th' dope on your big sister, Stella.

STELLA : Stanley, stop picking on Blanche.

STANLEY : That girl calls me common!

STELLA : Lately you been doing all you can think of to rub her the wrong way, Stanley, and Blanche is sensitive and you've got to realize that Blanche and I grew up under very different circumstances than you did.

STANLEY : So I been told. And told and told and told! You know she's been feeding us a pack of lies here?

STELLA : No, I don't, and—

STANLEY : Well, she has, however. But now the cat's out of the bag! I found out some things!

STELLA : What—things?

STANLEY : Things I already suspected. But now I got proof from the most reliable sources—which I have checked on!

[*Blanche is singing in the bathroom a saccharine popular ballad which is used contrapuntally with Stanley's speech.*]

STELLA : [*to Stanley*] Lower your voice!

STANLEY : Some canary-bird, huh!

STELLA : Now please tell me quietly what you think you've found out about my sister.

STANLEY : Lie Number One: All this squeamishness she puts on! You should just know the line she's been feeding to Mitch—He thought she had never been more than kissed by a fellow! But Sister Blanche is no lily! Ha-ha! Some lily she is!

STELLA : What have you heard and who from?

STANLEY : Our supply-man down at the plant has been going through Laurel for years and he knows all about her and everybody else in the town of Laurel knows all about her. She is as famous in Laurel as if she was the President of the United States, only she is not respected by any party! This supply-man stops at a hotel called the Flamingo.

BLANCHE : [*singing blithely*] "Say, it's only a paper moon, Sailing over a cardboard sea—But it wouldn't be make-believe If you believed in me!"

STELLA : What about the—Flamingo?

STANLEY : She stayed there, too.

STELLA : My sister lived at Belle Reve.

STANLEY : This is after the home-place had slipped through her lily white fingers! She moved to the Flamingo! A second class hotel which has the advantage of not interfering in the private social life of the personalities there! The Flamingo is used to all kinds of goings-on. But even the management of the Flamingo was impressed by Dame Blanche! In fact they were so impressed by Dame Blanche that they requested her to turn in her room-key—for permanently! This happened a couple of weeks before she showed here.

BLANCHE : [*singing*] "It's a Barnum and Bailey world. Just as phony as it can be—But it wouldn't be make-believe if you believed in me!"

STELLA : What—contemptible—lies!

STANLEY : Sure, I can see how you would be upset by this. She pulled the wool over your eyes as much as Mitch's!

STELLA : It's pure invention! There's not a word of truth in it and if I were a man and this creature had dared to invent such things in my presence—

BLANCHE : [*singing*] "Without your love, It's a honky-tonk parade! Without your love, It's a melody played, In a penny arcade..."

STANLEY : Honey, I told you I thoroughly checked on these stories! Now wait till I finish. The trouble with Dame Blanche was that she couldn't put on her act any more in Laurel! They got wised up after two or three dates with her and then they quit, and she goes on to another, the same old line, same old act, same old hooey! But the town was too small for this to go on forever! And as time went by she became a town character. Regarded as not just different but downright loco—nuts.

[*Stella draws back.*]

And for the last year or two she has been washed up like poison. That's why she's here this summer, visiting royalty, putting on all this act—because she's practically told by the mayor to get out of town! Yes, did you know there was an army camp near Laurel and your sister's was one of the places called "Out-of-Bounds"?

BLANCHE : "It's only a paper moon. Just as phony as it can be— But it wouldn't be make-believe, If you believed in me!"

STANLEY : Well, so much for her being such a refined and particular type of girl. Which brings us to Lie Number Two.

STELLA : I don't want to hear any more!

STANLEY : She's not going back to teach school! In fact I am willing to bet you that she never had no idea of returning to Laurel! She didn't resign temporarily from the high school because of her nerves! No, siree, Bob! She didn't. They locked her out of that high school before the spring term ended—and I hate to tell you the reason that step was taken! A seventeen-year-old boy—she'd gotten mixed up with!

BLANCHE : "It's a Barnum and Bailey world, Just as phony as it can be—"

[*In the bathroom the water goes on loud; little breathless cries and peals of laughter are heard as if a child were frolicking in the tub.*]

STELLA : This is making me—sick!

STANLEY : The boy's dad learned about it and got in touch with the high school superintendent. Boy, oh, boy, I'd like to have been in that office when Dame Blanche was called on the carpet! I'd like to have seen her trying to squirm out of that one! But they had her on the hook good and proper that time and she knew that the jig was all up! They told her she better move on to some fresh territory. Yep, it was practickly a town ordinance passed against her!

[*The bathroom door is opened and Blanche thrusts her head out, holding a towel about her hair.*]

BLANCHE : Stella!

STELLA : [*faintly*] Yes, Blanche?

BLANCHE : Give me another bath-towel to dry my hair with. I've just washed it.

STELLA : Yes, Blanche. [*She crosses in a dazed way from the kitchen to the bathroom door with a towel.*]

BLANCHE : What's the matter, honey?

STELLA : Matter? Why?

BLANCHE : You have such a strange expression on your face!

STELLA : Oh—[*She tries to laugh*] I guess I'm a little tired!

BLANCHE : Why don't you bathe, too, soon as I get out?

STANLEY : [*calling from the kitchen*] How soon is that going to be?

BLANCHE : Not so terribly long! Possess your soul in patience!

STANLEY : It's not my soul, it's my kidneys I'm worried about! [*Blanche slams the door. Stanley laughs harshly. Stella comes slowly back into the kitchen.*]

STANLEY : Well, what do you think of it?

STELLA : I don't believe all of those stories and I think your supply-man was mean and rotten to tell them. It's possible that some of the things he said are partly true. There are things about my sister I don't approve of—things that caused sorrow at home. She was always—flighty!

STANLEY : Flighty!

STELLA : But when she was young, very young, she married a boy who wrote poetry… He was extremely good-looking. I think Blanche didn't just love him but worshipped the ground he walked on! Adored him and thought him almost too fine to be human! But then she found out—

STANLEY : What?

STELLA : This beautiful and talented young man was a degenerate. Didn't your supply-man give you that information?

STANLEY : All we discussed was recent history. That must have been a pretty long time ago.

STELLA : Yes, it was—a pretty long time ago…

[*Stanley comes up and takes her by the shoulders rather gently. She gently withdraws from him. Automatically she starts sticking little pink candles in the birthday cake.*]

STANLEY : How many candles you putting in that cake?

STELLA : I'll stop at twenty-five.

STANLEY : Is company expected?

STELLA : We asked Mitch to come over for cake and ice cream.

[*Stanley looks a little uncomfortable. He lights a cigarette from the one he has just finished.*]

STANLEY : I wouldn't be expecting Mitch over tonight.

[*Stella pauses in her occupation with candles and looks slowly around at Stanley.*]

STELLA : Why?

STANLEY : Mitch is a buddy of mine. We were in the same outfit together—Two-forty-first Engineers. We work in the same plant and now on the same bowling team. You think I could face him if—

STELLA : Stanley Kowalski, did you—did you repeat what that—?

STANLEY : You're goddam right I told him! I'd have that on my conscience the rest of my life if I knew all that stuff and let my best friend get caught!

STELLA : Is Mitch through with her?

STANLEY : Wouldn't you be if—?

STELLA : I said, Is Mitch through with her?

[*Blanche's voice is lifted again, serenely as a bell. She sings "But it wouldn't be make-believe if you believed in me."*]

STANLEY : No, I don't think he's necessarily through with her—just wised up!

STELLA : Stanley, she thought Mitch was—going to—going to marry her. I was hoping so, too.

STANLEY : Well, he's not going to marry her. Maybe he was, but he's not going to jump in a tank with a school of sharks—now! [*He rises*] Blanche! Oh, Blanche! Can I please get in my bathroom? [*There is a pause.*]

BLANCHE : Yes, indeed, sir! Can you wait one second while I dry?

STANLEY : Having waited one hour I guess one second ought to pass in a hurry.

STELLA : And she hasn't got her job? Well, what will she do!

STANLEY : She's not stayin' here after Tuesday. You know that, don't you? Just to make sure I bought her ticket myself. A bus ticket!

STELLA : In the first place, Blanche wouldn't go on a bus.

STANLEY : She'll go on a bus and like it.

STELLA : No, she won't, no, she won't, Stanley!

STANLEY : She'll go! Period. P.S. She'll go Tuesday!

STELLA : [*slowly*] What'll—she—do? What on earth will she—do!

STANLEY : Her future is mapped out for her.

STELLA : What do you mean?

[*Blanche sings.*]

STANLEY : Hey, canary bird! Toots! Get OUT of the BATHROOM!

[*The bathroom door flies open and Blanche emerges with a gay peal of laughter, but as Stanley crosses past her, a frightened look appears on her face, almost a look of panic. He doesn't look at her but slams the bathroom door shut as he goes in.*]

BLANCHE : [*snatching up a hairbrush*] Oh, I feel so good after my long, hot bath, I feel so good and cool and—rested!

STELLA : [*sadly and doubtfully from the kitchen*] Do you, Blanche?

BLANCHE : [*brushing her hair vigorously*] Yes, I do, so refreshed! [*She tinkles her highball glass.*] A hot bath and a long, cold drink always give me a brand new outlook on life! [*She looks through the portieres at Stella, standing between them, and slowly stops brushing*] Something has happened!—What is it?

STELLA : [*fuming away quickly*] Why, nothing has happened, Blanche.

BLANCHE : You're lying! Something has!

[*She stares fearfully at Stella, who pretends to be busy at the table. The distant piano goes into a hectic breakdown.*]

Scene 8

Three-quarters of an hour later. The view through the big windows is fading gradually into a still-golden dusk. A torch of sunlight blazes on the side of a big water-tank or oil-drum across the empty lot toward the business district which is now pierced by pinpoints of lighted windows or windows reflecting the sunset. The three people are completing a dismal birthday supper. Stanley looks sullen. Stella is embarrassed and sad. Blanche has a tight, artificial smile on her drawn face. There is a fourth place at the table which is left vacant.

BLANCHE : [*suddenly*] Stanley, tell us a joke, tell us a funny story to make us all laugh. I don't know what's the matter, we're all so solemn. Is it because I've been stood up by my beau?

[*Stella laughs feebly.*]

It's the first time in my entire experience with men, and I've had a good deal of all sorts, that I've actually been stood up by anybody! Ha-ha! I don't know how to take it… Tell us a funny little story, Stanley! Something to help us out.

STANLEY : I didn't think you liked my stories, Blanche.

BLANCHE : I like them when they're amusing but not indecent.

STANLEY : I don't know any refined enough for your taste.

BLANCHE : Then let me tell one.

STELLA : Yes, you tell one, Blanche. You used to know lots of good stories.

[*The music fades.*]

BLANCHE : Let me see, now... I must run through my repertoire! Oh. yes—I love parrot stories! Do you all like parrot stories? Well, this one's about the old maid and the parrot. This old maid, she had a parrot that cursed a blue streak and knew more vulgar expressions than Mr. Kowalski!

STANLEY : Huh.

BLANCHE : And the only way to hush the parrot up was to put the cover back on its cage so it would think it was night and go back to sleep. Well, one morning the old maid had just uncovered the parrot for the day—when who should she see coming up the front walk but the preacher! Well, she rushed back to the parrot and slipped the cover back on the cage and then she let in the preacher. And the parrot was perfectly still, just as quiet as a mouse, but just as she was asking the preacher how much sugar he wanted in his coffee—the parrot broke the silence with a loud—[*She whistles*]—and said—"God damn, but that was a short day!"

[*She throws back her head and laughs. Stella also makes an ineffectual effort to seem amused. Stanley pays no attention to the story but reaches way aver the table to spear his fork into the remaining chop which he eats with his fingers.*]

BLANCHE : Apparently Mr. Kowalski was not amused.

STELLA : Mr. Kowalski is too busy making a pig of himself to think of anything else!

STANLEY : That's right, baby.

STELLA : Your face and your fingers are disgustingly greasy. Go and wash up and then help me clear the table.

[*He hurls a plate to the floor.*]

STANLEY : That's how I'll clear the table! [*He seizes her arm*] Don't ever talk that way to me! "Pig—Polack—disgusting—vulgar—greasy!"—them kind of words have been on your tongue and your sister's too much around here! What do you two think you are? A pair of queens? Remember what Huey Long said—"Every Man is a King!" And I am the king around here, so don't forget it! [*He hurls a cup and saucer to the floor*] My place is cleared! You want me to clear your places?

[*Stella begins to cry weakly. Stanley stalks out on the porch and lights a cigarette.*]

[*The Negro entertainers around the corner are heard.*]

BLANCHE : What happened while I was bathing? What did he tell you, Stella?

STELLA : Nothing, nothing, nothing!

BLANCHE : I think he told you something about Mitch and me! You know why Mitch didn't come but you won't tell me! [*Stella shakes her head helplessly*] I'm going to call him!

STELLA : I wouldn't call him, Blanche.

BLANCHE : I am, I'm going to call him on the phone.

STELLA : [*miserably*] I wish you wouldn't.

BLANCHE : I intend to be given some explanation from someone!

[*She rushes to the phone in the bedroom. Stella goes out on the porch and stares reproachfully at her husband. He grunts and turns away from her.*]

STELLA : I hope you're pleased with your doings. I never had so much trouble swallowing food in my life, looking at that girl's face and the empty chair! [*She cries quietly.*]

BLANCHE : [*at the phone*] Hello. Mr. Mitchell, please… Oh… I would like to leave a number if I may. Magnolia 9047. And say it's important to call… Yes, very important… Thank you. [*She remains by the phone with a lost, frightened look.*]

[*Stanley turns slowly back toward his wife and takes her clumsily in his arms.*]

STANLEY : Stell, it's gonna be all right after she goes and after you've had the baby. It's gonna be all right again between you and me the way that it was. You remember that way that it was? Them nights we had together? God, honey, it's gonna be sweet when we can make noise in the night the way that we used to and get the colored lights going with nobody's sister behind the curtains to hear us!

[*Their upstairs neighbors are heard in bellowing laughter at something. Stanley chuckles.*] Steve an' Eunice…

STELLA : Come on back in. [*She returns to the kitchen and starts lighting the candles on the white cake.*] Blanche?

BLANCHE : Yes. [*She returns from the bedroom to the table in the kitchen.*] Oh, those pretty little candles! Oh, don't burn them, Stella.

STELLA : I certainly will.

[*Stanley comes back in.*]

BLANCHE : You ought to save them for baby's birthdays. Oh, I hope candles are going to glow in his life and I hope that his eyes are going to be like candles, like two blue candles lighted in a white cake!

STANLEY : [*sitting down*] What poetry!

BLANCHE : [*she pauses reflectively for a moment*] I shouldn't have called him.

STELLA : There's lots of things could have happened.

BLANCHE : There's no excuse for it, Stella. I don't have to put up with insults. I won't be taken for granted.

STANLEY : Goddam, it's hot in here with the steam from the bathroom.

BLANCHE : I've said I was sorry three times. [*The piano fades out.*] I take hot baths for my nerves. Hydro-therapy, they call it. You healthy Polack, without a nerve in your body, of course you don't know what anxiety feels like!

STANLEY : I am not a Polack. People from Poland are Poles, not Polacks. But what I am is a one hundred percent American, born and raised in the greatest country on earth and proud as hell of it, so don't ever call me a Polack.

[*The phone rings. Blanche rises expectantly.*]

BLANCHE : Oh, that's for me, I'm sure.

STANLEY : *I'm* not sure. Keep your seat. [*He crosses leisurely to phone.*] H'lo. Aw, yeh, hello, Mac.

[*He leans against wall, staring insultingly in at Blanche. She sinks back in her chair with a frightened look. Stella leans over and touches her shoulder.*]

BLANCHE : Oh, keep your hands on me, Stella. What is the matter with you? Why do you look at me with that pitying look?

STANLEY : [*bawling*] QUIET IN THERE!—We've got a noisy woman on the place.—Go on, Mac. At Riley's? No, I don't want a bowl at Riley's. I had a little trouble with Riley last week. I'm the team-captain, ain't I? All right, then, we're not gonna bowl at Riley's, we're gonna bowl at the West Side or the Gala! All right, Mac. See you!

[*He hangs up and returns to the table. Blanche fiercely controls herself, drinking quickly from her tumbler of water. He doesn't look at her but reaches in a pocket. Then he speaks slowly and with false amiability.*]

Sister Blanche, I've got a little birthday remembrance for you.

BLANCHE : Oh, have you, Stanley? I wasn't expecting any, I—I don't know why Stella wants to observe my birthday! I'd much rather forget it—when you—reach twenty-seven! Well—age is a subject that you'd prefer to—ignore!

STANLEY : Twenty-seven?

BLANCHE : [*quickly*] What is it? Is it for me?

[*He is holding a little envelope toward her.*]

STANLEY : Yes, I hope you like it!

BLANCHE : Why, why—Why, it's a—

STANLEY : Ticket! Back to Laurel! On the Greyhound! Tuesday!

[*The Varsouviana music steals in softly and continues playing. Stella rises abruptly and turns her back. Blanche tries to smile. Then she tries to laugh. Then she gives both up and springs from the table and runs into the next room. She clutches her throat and then runs into the bathroom. Coughing, gagging sounds are heard.*]

Well!

STELLA : You didn't need to do that.

STANLEY : Don't forget all that I took off her.

STELLA : You needn't have been so cruel to someone alone as she is.

STANLEY : Delicate piece she is.

STELLA : She is. She was. You didn't know Blanche as a girl. Nobody, nobody, was tender and trusting as she was But people like you abused her, and forced her to change.

[He crosses into the bedroom, ripping off his shirt, and changes into a brilliant silk bowling shirt. She follows him.]

Do you think you're going bowling now?

STANLEY : Sure.

STELLA : You're not going bowling. [*She catches hold of his shirt*] Why did you do this to her?

STANLEY : I done nothing to no one. Let go of my shirt. You've torn it.

STELLA : I want to know why. Tell me why.

STANLEY : When we first met, me and you, you thought I was common. How right you was, baby. I was common as dirt. You showed me the snapshot of the place with the columns. I pulled you down off them columns and how you loved it, having them colored lights going! And wasn't we happy together, wasn't it all okay till she showed here?

[Stella makes a slight movement. Her look goes suddenly inward as if some interior voice had called her name. She begins a slow, shuffling progress from the bedroom to the kitchen, leaning and resting on the back of the chair and then on the edge of a table with a blind look and listening expression. Stanley, finishing with his shirt, is unaware of her reaction.]

And wasn't we happy together? Wasn't it all okay? Till she showed here. Hoity-toity, describing me as an ape. [*He suddenly notices the change in Stella*] Hey, what is it, Stella?

[He crosses to her.]

STELLA : [*quietly*] Take me to the hospital.

[*He is with her now, supporting her with his arm, murmuring indistinguishably as they go outside.*]

Scene 9

A while later that evening—Blanche is seated in a tense hunched position in a bedroom chair that she has re-covered with diagonal green-and-white stripes. She has on her scarlet satin robe. On the table beside chair is a bottle of liquor and a glass. The rapid, feverish polka tune, the "Varsouviana," is heard. The music is in her mind; she is drinking to escape it and the sense of disaster closing in on her, and she seems to whisper the words of the song. An electric fan is turning back and forth across her. Mitch comes around the corner in work clothes: blue denim shirt and pants. He is unshaven. He climbs the steps to the door and rings. Blanche is startled.

BLANCHE : Who is it, please?

MITCH : [*hoarsely*] Me. Mitch.

[*The polka tune stops.*]

BLANCHE : Mitch!—just a minute.

[*She rushes about frantically, hiding the bottle in a closet, crouching at the mirror and dabbing her face with cologne and powder. She is so excited her breath is audible as she dashes about. At last she rushes to the door in the kitchen and lets him in.*]

Mitch!—Y'know, I really shouldn't let you in after the treatment I have received from you this evening! So utterly uncavalier! But hello, beautiful!

[*She offers him her lips. He ignores it and pushes past her into the flat. She looks fearfully after him as he stalks into the bedroom.*]

My, my, what a cold shoulder! And such uncouth apparel! Why, you haven't even shaved! The unforgivable insult to a lady! But I forgive you. I forgive you because it's such a relief to see you. You've stopped that polka tune that I had caught in my head. Have you ever had anything caught in your head? No, of course you haven't, you dumb angel-puss, you'd never get anything awful caught in your head!

[*He stares at her while she follows him while she talks. It is obvious that he has had a few drinks on the way over.*]

MITCH : Do we have to have that fan on?

BLANCHE : No!

MITCH : I don't like fans.

BLANCHE : Then let's turn it off, honey. I'm not partial to them!

[*She presses the switch and the fan nods slowly off. She clears her throat uneasily as Mitch plumps himself down on the bed in the bedroom and lights a cigarette.] I don't know what there is to drink. I—haven't investigated.*]

MITCH : I don't want Stan's liquor.

BLANCHE : It isn't Stan's. Everything here isn't Stan's. Some things on the premises are actually mine! How is your mother? Isn't your mother well?

MITCH : Why?

BLANCHE : Something's the matter tonight, but never mind. I won't cross-examine the witness. I'll just—[*She touches her forehead vaguely. The polka tune starts up again.*]—

pretend I don't notice anything different about you! That—music again...

MITCH : What music?

BLANCHE : The "Varaouviana"! The polka tune they were playing when Allan—Wait!

[*A distant revolver shot is heard. Blanche seems relieved.*]

There now, the shot! It always stops after that.

[*The polka music dies out again.*]

Yes, now it's stopped.

MITCH : Are you boxed out of your mind?

BLANCHE : I'll go and see what I can find in the way of—[*She crosses into the closet, pretending to search for the bottle.*] Oh, by the way, excuse me for not being dressed. But I'd practically given you up! Had you forgotten your invitation to supper?

MITCH : I wasn't going to see you anymore.

BLANCHE : Wait a minute. I can't hear what you're saying and you talk so little that when you do say something, I don't want to miss a single syllable of it... What am I looking around here for? Oh, yes—liquor! We've had so much excitement around here this evening that I am boxed out of my mind! [*She pretends suddenly to find the bottle. He draws his foot up on the bed and stares at her contemptuously.*] Here's something. Southern Comfort! What is that, I wonder?

MITCH : If you don't know, it must belong to Stan.

BLANCHE : Take your foot off the bed. It has a light cover on it. Of course you boys don't notice things like that. I've done so much with this place since I've been here.

MITCH : I bet you have.

BLANCHE : You saw it before I came. Well, look at it now! This room is almost—dainty! I want to keep it that way. I wonder if this stuff ought to be mixed with something? Ummm, it's sweet, so sweet! It's terribly, terribly sweet! Why, it's a liqueur, I believe! Yes, that's what it is, a liqueur! [*Mitch grunts.*] I'm afraid you won't like it, but try it, and maybe you will.

MITCH : I told you already I don't want none of his liquor and I mean it. You ought to lay off his liquor. He says you been lapping it up all summer like a wildcat!

BLANCHE : What a fantastic statement! Fantastic of him to say it, fantastic of you to repeat it! I won't descend to the level of such cheap accusations to answer them, even!

MITCH : Huh.

BLANCHE : What's in your mind? I see something in your eyes!

MITCH : [*getting up*] It's dark in here.

BLANCHE : I like it dark. The dark is comforting to me.

MITCH : I don't think I ever seen you in the light. [*Blanche laughs breathlessly*] That's a fact!

BLANCHE : Is it?

MITCH : I've never seen you in the afternoon.

BLANCHE : Whose fault is that?

MITCH : You never want to go out in the afternoon.

BLANCHE : Why, Mitch, you're at the plant in the afternoon!

MITCH : Not Sunday afternoon. I've asked you to go out with me sometimes on Sundays but you always make an excuse. You never want to go out till after six and then it's always some place that's not lighted much.

BLANCHE : There is some obscure meaning in this but I fail to catch it.

MITCH : What it means is I've never had a real good look at you, Blanche. Let's turn the light on here.

BLANCHE : [*fearfully*] Light? Which light? What for?

MITCH : This one with the paper thing on it. [*He tears the paper lantern off the light bulb. She utters a frightened gasp.*]

BLANCHE : What did you do that for?

MITCH : So I can take a look at you good and plain!

BLANCHE : Of course you don't really mean to be insulting!

MITCH : No, just realistic.

BLANCHE : I don't want realism. I want magic! [*Mitch laughs*] Yes, yes, magic! I try to give that to people. I misrepresent things to them. I don't tell truth, I tell what ought to be truth. And if that is sinful, then let me be damned for it!—*Don't turn the light on*!

[*Mitch crosses to the switch. He turns the light on and stares at her. She cries out and covers her face. He turns the light off again.*]

MITCH : [*slowly and bitterly*] I don't mind you being older than what I thought. But all the rest of it—Christ! That pitch about your ideals being so old-fashioned and all the malarkey that you've dished out all summer. Oh, I knew you weren't sixteen any more. But I was a fool enough to believe you was straight.

BLANCHE : Who told you I wasn't—'straight'? My loving brother-in-law. And you believed him.

MITCH : I called him a liar at first And then I checked on the story. First I asked our supply-man who travels through Laure. And then I talked directly over long-distance to this merchant.

BLANCHE : Who is this merchant?

MITCH : Kiefaber.

BLANCHE : The merchant Kiefaber of Laurel! I know the man. He whistled at me. I put him in his place. So now for revenge he makes up stories about me.

MITCH : Three people, Kiefaber, Stanley and Shaw, swore to them!

BLANCHE : Rub-a-dub-dub, three men in a tub! And such a filthy tub!

MITCH : Didn't you stay at a hotel called the Flamingo?

BLANCHE : Flamingo? No! Tarantula was the name of it! I stayed at a hotel called the Tarantula Arms!

MITCH : [*stupidly*] Tarantula?

BLANCHE : Yes, a big spider! That's where I brought my victims. [*She pours herself another drink*] Yes, I had many intimacies with strangers. After the death of Allan—intimacies with strangers was all I seemed able to fill my empty heart with… I think it was panic, just panic, that drove me from one to another, hunting for some protection—here and there, in the most—unlikely places—even, at last, in a seventeen-year-old boy but—somebody wrote the superintendent about it—"This woman is morally unfit for her position!"

[*She throws back her head with convulsive, sobbing laughter. Then she repeats the statement, gasps, and drinks.*]

True? Yes, I suppose—unfit somehow—anyway... So I came here. There was nowhere else I could go. I was played out. You know what played out is? My youth was suddenly gone up the water-spout, and—I met you. You said you needed somebody. Well, I needed somebody, too. I thanked God for you, because you seemed to be gentle—a cleft in the rock of the world that I could hide in! But I guess I was asking, hoping—too much! Kiefaber, Stanley and Shaw have tied an old tin can to the tail of the kite.

[*There is a pause. Mitch stares at her dumbly.*]

MITCH : You lied to me, Blanche.

BLANCHE : Don't say I lied to you.

MITCH : Lies, lies, inside and out, all lies.

BLANCHE : Never inside, I didn't lie in my heart…

[A Vendor comes around the corner. She is a blind Mexican woman in a dark shawl, carrying bunches of those gaudy tin flowers that lower class Mexicans display at funerals and other festive occasions. She is calling barely audibly. Her figure is only faintly visible outside the building.]

MEXICAN W.: Flores. Flores. Flores para los muertos. Flores. Flores.

BLANCHE : What? Oh! Somebody outside… [*She goes to the door. opens it and stares at the Mexican Woman.*]

MEXICAN W.: [*she is at the door and offers Blanche some of her flowers*] Flores? Flores para los muertos?

BLANCHE : [*frightened*] No, no! Not now! Not now!

[*She darts back into the apartment, slamming the door.*]

MEXICAN W.: [*she turns away and starts to move down the street*] Flores para los muertos.

[*The polka tune fades in.*]

BLANCHE : [*as if to herself*] Crumble and fade and—regrets—recriminations… "If you'd done this, it wouldn't've cost me that!"

MEXICAN W.: Corones para los muertos. Corones…

BLANCHE : Legacies! Huh… And other things such as bloodstained pillow-slips—"Her linen needs changing"—"Yes Mother." But couldn't we get a colored girl to do it?" No, we couldn't of course. Everything gone but the—

MEXICAN W.: Flores,

BLANCHE : Death—I used to sit here and she used to sit over there and death was as close as you are… We didn't dare even admit we had ever heard of it!

MEXICAN W.: Flores para los muertos, flores—flores…

BLANCHE : The opposite is desire. So do you wonder? How could you possibly wonder! Not far from Belle Reve, before we had lost Belle Reve, was a camp where they trained young soldiers. On Saturday nights they would go in town to get drunk—

MEXICAN W.: [*softly*] Corones…

BLANCHE : —and on the way back they would stagger onto my lawn and call—"Blanche! Blanche!"—The deaf old lady remaining suspected nothing. But sometimes I slipped outside to answer their calls… Later the paddy-wagon would gather them up like daisies… the long way home…

[*The Mexican Woman turns slowly and drifts back off with her soft mournful cries. Blanche goes to the dresser and leans forward on it. After a moment, Mitch rises and follows her purposefully. The polka music fades away. He places his hands on her waist and tries to turn her about.*]

BLANCHE : What do you want?

MITCH : [*fumbling to embrace her*] What I been missing all summer.

BLANCHE : Then marry me, Mitch!

MITCH : I don't think I want to marry you anymore.

BLANCHE : No?

MITCH : [*dropping his hands from her waist*] You're not clean enough to bring in the house with my mother.

BLANCHE : Go away, then. [He stares at her] Get out of here quick before I start screaming fire! [*Her throat is tightening with hysteria*] Get out of here quick before I start screaming fire. [*He still remains staring. She suddenly rushes to the big window with its pale blue square of the soft summer light and cries wildly.*]

Fire! Fire! Fire!

[*With a startled, gasp, Mitch turns and goes out the outer door, clatters awkwardly down the steps and around the corner of the building, Blanche staggers back from the window and falls to her knees. The distant piano is slow and blue.*]

Scene 10

It is a few hows later that night. Blanche has been drinking fairly steadily since Mitch left. She has dragged her wardrobe trunk into the center of the bedroom. It hangs open with flowery dresses thrown across it. As the drinking and packing went on, a mood of hysterical exhilaration came into her and she has decked herself out in a somewhat soiled and crumpled white satin evening gown and a pair of scuffed silver slippers with brilliants set in their heels. Now she is placing the rhinestone tiara on her head before the mirror of the dressing-table and murmuring excitedly as if to a group of spectral admirers.

BLANCHE : How about taking a swim, a moonlight swim at the old rock quarry? If anyone's sober enough to drive a car! Ha-ha! Best way in the world to stop your head buzzing! Only you've got to be careful to dive where the deep pool is—if you hit a rock you don't come up till tomorrow...

[*Tremblingly she lifts the hand mirror for a closer inspection. She catches her breath and slams the mirror face down with such violence that the glass cracks. She moans a little and attempts to rise.*

[*Stanley appears around the corner of the building. He still has on the vivid green silk bowling shirt. As he rounds the corner the honky-tonk music is heard. It continues softly throughout the scene.*]

[*He enters the kitchen, slamming the door. As he peers in at Blanche, he gives a low whistle. He has had a few drinks on the way and has brought some quart beer bottles home with him.*]

BLANCHE : How is my sister?

STANLEY : She is doing okay.

BLANCHE : And how is the baby?

STANLEY : [*grinning amiably*] The baby won't come before morning so they told me to go home and get a little shuteye.

BLANCHE : Does that mean we are to be alone in here?

STANLEY : Yep. Just me and you, Blanche. Unless you got somebody hid under the bed. What've you got on those fine feathers for?

BLANCHE : Oh, that's right. You left before my wire came.

STANLEY : You got a wire?

BLANCHE : I received a telegram from an old admirer of mine.

STANLEY : Anything good?

BLANCHE : I think so. An invitation.

STANLEY : What to? A fireman's ball?

BLANCHE : [*throwing back her head*] A cruise of the Caribbean on a yacht!

STANLEY : Well, well. What do you know?

BLANCHE : I have never been so surprised in my life.

STANLEY : I guess not.

BLANCHE : It came like a bolt from the blue!

STANLEY : Who did you say it was from?

BLANCHE : An old beau of mine.

STANLEY : The one that give you the white fox-pieces?

BLANCHE : Mr. Shep Huntleigh. I wore his ATO pin my last year at college. I hadn't seen him again until last Christmas. I ran into him on Biscayne Boulevard. Then—just now—this wire—inviting me on a cruise of the Caribbean! The problem is clothes. I tore into my trunk to see what I have that's suitable for the tropics!

STANLEY : And come up with that—gorgeous—diamond—tiara?

BLANCHE : This old relic? Ha-ha! It's only rhinestones.

STANLEY : Gosh. I thought it was Tiffany diamonds. [*He unbuttons his shirt.*]

BLANCHE : Well, anyhow, I shall be entertained in style.

STANLEY : Uh-huh. It goes to show, you never know what is coming.

BLANCHE : Just when I thought my luck had begun to fail me—

STANLEY : Into the picture pops this Miami millionaire.

BLANCHE : This man is not from Miami. This man is from Dallas.

STANLEY : This man is from Dallas?

BLANCHE : Yes, this man is from Dallas where gold spouts out of the ground!

STANLEY : Well, just so he's from somewhere! [*He starts removing his shirt.*]

BLANCHE : Close the curtains before you undress any further.

STANLEY : [*amiably*] This is all I'm going to undress right now. [*He rips the sack off a quart beer bottle*] Seen a bottle opener?

[*She moves slowly toward the dresser, where she stands with her hands knotted together.*]

I used to have a cousin who could open a beer bottle with his teeth. [*Pounding the bottle cap on the corner of table*] That was his only accomplishment, all he could do—he was just a human bottle-opener. And then one time, at a wedding party, he broke his front teeth off! After that he was so ashamed of himself he used t' sneak out of the house when company came...

[*The bottle cap pops off and a geyser of foam shoots up. Stanley laughs happily, holding up the bottle over his head.*] Ha-ha! Rain from heaven! [*He extends the bottle toward her*] Shall we bury the hatchet and make it a loving-cup? Huh?

BLANCHE : No, thank you.

STANLEY : Well, it's a red letter night for us both. You having an oil millionaire and me having a baby.

[*He goes to the bureau in the bedroom and crouches to remove something from the bottom drawer.*]

BLANCHE : [*drawing back*] What are you doing in here?

STANLEY : Here's something I always break out on special occasions like this. The silk pyjamas I wore on my wedding night!

BLANCHE : Oh.

STANLEY : When the telephone rings and they say, "You've got a son!" Ill tear this off and wave it like a flag! [*He shakes out a brilliant pyjama coat*] I guess we are both entitled to put on the dog. [*He goes back to the kitchen with the coat over his arm.*]

BLANCHE : When I think of how divine it is going to be to have such a thing as privacy once more—I could weep with joy!

STANLEY : This millionaire from Dallas is not going to interfere with your privacy any?

BLANCHE : It won't be the sort of thing you have in mind. This man is a gentleman and he respects me. [*Improvising feverishly*] What he wants is my companionship. Having great wealth sometimes makes people lonely! A cultivated woman, a woman of intelligence and breeding, can enrich a man's life—immeasurably! I have those things to offer, and this doesn't take them away. Physical beauty is passing. A transitory possession. But beauty of the mind and richness of the spirit and tenderness of the heart—and I have all of those things—aren't taken away, but grow! Increase with the years! How strange that I should be called a destitute woman! When I have all of these treasures locked in my heart. [*A choked sob comes from her*] I think of myself as a very, very rich woman! But I have been foolish—casting my pearls before swine!

STANLEY : Swine, huh?

BLANCHE : Yes, swine! Swine! And I'm thinking not only of you but of your friend, Mr. Mitchell. He came to see me tonight. He dared to come here in his work-clothes! And to repeat slander to me, vicious stories that he had gotten from you! I gave him his walking papers…

STANLEY : You did, huh?

BLANCHE : But then he came back. He returned with a box of roses to beg my forgiveness! He implored my forgiveness. But some things are not forgivable. Deliberate cruelty is not forgivable. It is the one unforgivable thing in my opinion and it is the one thing of which I have never, never been guilty. And so I told him, I said to him, "Thank you," but it was foolish of me to think that we could ever adapt ourselves to each other. Our ways of life are too different. Our attitudes and our backgrounds are incompatible. We have to be realistic about such things. So farewell, my friend! And let there be no hard feelings…

STANLEY : Was this before or after the telegram came from the Texas oil millionaire?

BLANCHE : What telegram! No! No, after! As a matter of fact, the wire came just as—

STANLEY : As a matter of fact there wasn't no wire at all!

BLANCHE : Oh, oh!

STANLEY : There isn't no millionaire! And Mitch didn't come back; with roses 'cause I know where he is—

BLANCHE : Oh!

STANLEY : There isn't a goddam thing but imagination!

BLANCHE : Oh!

STANLEY : And lies and conceit and tricks!

BLANCHE : Oh!

STANLEY : And look at yourself! Take a look at yourself in that wornout Mardi Gras outfit, rented for fifty cents from some ragpicker! And with the crazy crown on! What queen do you think you are?

BLANCHE : Oh—God…

STANLEY : I've been on to you from the start! Not once did you pull any wool over this boy's eyes! You come in here and sprinkle the place with powder and spray perfume and cover the light bulb with a paper lantern, and lo and behold the place has turned into Egypt and you are the Queen of the Nile! Sitting on your throne and swilling down my liquor! I say—Ha!—Ha! Do you hear me? Ha—ha—ha! [*He walks into the bedroom.*]

BLANCHE : Don't come in here!

[*Lurid reflections appear on the wall around Blanche. The shadows are of a grotesque and menacing form. She catches her breath, crosses to the phone and jiggles the hook. Stanley goes into the bathroom and closes the door.*]

Operator, operator! Give me long-distance, please… I want to get in touch with Mr. Shep Huntleigh of Dallas. He's so well-known he doesn't require any address. Just ask anybody who—Wait! I—No, I couldn't find it right now… Please understand, I—No! No, wait!... One moment! Someone is—Nothing! Hold on, please!

[*She sets the phone down and crosses warily into the kitchen. The night is filled with inhuman voices like cries in a jungle.*]

[*The shadows and lurid reflections move sinously as flames along the wall spaces.*]

[*Through the back wall of the rooms, which have become transparent, can be seen the sidewalk. A prostitute has rolled a drunkard. He pursues her along the walk, overtakes her and there is a struggle. A policeman's whistle breaks it up. The figures disappear.*]

[*Some moments later the Negro Woman appears around the corner with a sequined bag which the prostitute had dropped on the walk. She is rooting excitedly through it.*]

[*Blanche presses her knuckles to her lips and returns slowly to the phone. She speaks in a hoarse whisper.*]

BLANCHE : Operator! Operator! Never mind long-distance. Get Western Union. There isn't time to be—Western—Western Union! [*She waits anxiously.*]

Western Union? Yes! I—want to—Take down this message! "In desperate, desperate circumstances! Help me! Caught in a trap. Caught in—"Oh!

[*The bathroom door is thrown open and Stanley comes out in the brilliant silk pyjamas. He grins at her as he knots the tasseled sash about his waist. She gasps and backs away from the phone. He stares at her for a count of ten.*

Then a clicking becomes audible from the telephone, steady and rasping.]

STANLEY : You left th' phone off th' hook.

[*He crosses to it deliberately and sets it back on the hook. After he has replaced it, he stares at her again, his mouth slowly curving into a grin, as he weaves between Blanche and the outer door.*]

[*The barely audible "blue piano" begins to drum up louder. The sound of it turns into the roar of an approaching locomotive. Blanche crouches, pressing her fists to her ears until it has gone by.*]

BLANCHE : [*finally straightening*] Let me—let me get by you!

STANLEY : Get by me! Sure. Go ahead. [*He moves back a pace in the doorway.*]

BLANCHE : You—you stand over there! [*She indicates a further position.*]

STANLEY : [*grinning*] You got plenty of room to walk by me now.

BLANCHE : Not with you there! But I've got to get out somehow!

STANLEY : You think I'll interfere with you? Ha-ha!

[*The "blue piano" goes softly. She turns confusedly and makes a faint gesture. The inhuman jungle voices rise up. He takes a step toward her, biting his tongue which protrudes between his lips.*]

STANLEY : [*softly*] Come to think of it—maybe you wouldn't be bad to—interfere with…

[*Blanche moves backward through the door into the bedroom.*]

BLANCHE : Stay back! Don't you come toward me another step or I'll—

STANLEY : What?

BLANCHE : Some awful thing will happen! It will!

STANLEY : What are you putting on now?

[*They are now both inside the bedroom.*]

BLANCHE : I warn you, don't, I'm in danger!

[*He takes another step. She smashes a bottle on the table and faces him, clutching the broken top.*]

STANLEY : What did you do that for?

BLANCHE : So I could twist the broken end in your face!

STANLEY : I bet you would do that!

BLANCHE : I would! I will if you—

STANLEY : Oh! So you want some rough-house! All right, let's have some rough-house!

[*He springs toward her, overturning the table. She cries out and strikes at him with the bottle top but he catches her wrist.*]

Tiger—tiger! Drop the bottle top! Drop it! We've had this date with each other from the beginning!

[*She moans. The bottle top falls. She sinks to her knees. He picks up her inert figure and carries her to the bed. The hot trumpet and drums from the Four Deuces sound loudly.*]

Scene 11

It is some weeks later. Stella is packing Blanche's things. Sounds of water can be heard running in the bathroom. The portieres are partly open on the poker players—Stanley, Steve, Mitch and Pablo—who sit around the table in the kitchen. The atmosphere of the kitchen is now the same raw, lurid one of the disastrous poker night. The building is framed by the sky of turquoise. Stella has been crying as she arranges the flowery dresses in the open trunk. Eunice comes down the steps from her flat above and enters the kitchen. There is an outburst from the poker table.

STANLEY : Drew to an inside straight and made it, by God.

PABLO : Maldita sea to suerte!

STANLEY : Put it in English, greaseball!

PABLO : I am cursing your rutting luck.

STANLEY : [*prodigiously elated*] You know what luck is? Luck is believing you're lucky. Take at Salerno. I believed I was lucky. I figured that 4 out of 5 would not come through but I would... and I did. I put that down as a rule. To hold front position in this rat-race you've got to believe you are lucky.

MITCH : You... you... you... Brag... brag... bull... bull. [*Stella goes into the bedroom and starts folding a dress.*]

STANLEY : What's the matter with him?

EUNICE : [*walking past the table*] I always did say that men are callous things with no feelings, but this does beat anything. Making pigs of yourselves. [*She comes through the portieres into the bedroom.*]

STANLEY : What's the matter with her?

STELLA : How is my baby?

EUNICE : Sleeping like a little angel. Brought you some grapes. [*She puts them on a stool and lowers her voice.*] Blanche?

STELLA : Bathing.

EUNICE : How is she?

STELLA : She wouldn't eat anything but asked for a drink.

EUNICE : What did you tell her?

STELLA : I—just told her that—we'd made arrangements for her to rest in the country. She's got it mixed in her mind with Shep Huntleigh.

[*Blanche opens the bathroom door slightly.*]

BLANCHE : Stella.

STELLA : Yes, Blanche?

BLANCHE : If anyone calls while I'm bathing take the number and tell them I'll call right back.

STELLA : Yes.

BLANCHE : That cool yellow silk—the boucle. See if it's crushed. If it's not too crushed I'll wear it and on the lapel that silver and turquoise pin in the shape of a seahorse. You will find them in the heart-shaped box I keep my accessories in. And Stella... Try and locate a bunch of artificial violets in that box, too, to pin with the seahorse on the lapel of the jacket.

[*She closes the door. Stella turns to Eunice.*]

STELLA : I don't know if I did the right thing.

EUNICE : What else could you do?

STELLA : I couldn't believe her story and go on living with Stanley.

EUNICE : Don't ever believe it. Life has got to go on. No matter what happens, you've got to keep on going.

[*The bathroom door opens a little.*]

BLANCHE : [*looking out*] Is the coast clear?

STELLA : Yes, Blanche. [*To Eunice*] Tell her how well she's looking.

BLANCHE : Please close the curtains before I come out.

STELLA : They're closed.

STANLEY : —How many for you?

PABLO : —Two.

STEVE : —Three.

[*Blanche appears in the amber tight of the door. She has a tragic radiance in her red satin robe following the sculptural lines of her body. The "Varsouviana" rises audibly as Blanche enters the bedroom.*]

BLANCHE : [*with faintly hysterical vivacity*] I have just washed my hair.

STELLA : Did you?

BLANCHE : I'm not sure I got the soap out.

EUNICE : Such fine hair!

BLANCHE : [*accepting the compliment*] It's a problem. Didn't I get a call?

STELLA : Who from, Blanche?

BLANCHE : Shep Huntleigh…

STELLA : Why, not yet, honey!

BLANCHE : How strange! I—

[At the sound of Blanche's voice Mitch's arm supporting his cards has sagged and his gaze is dissolved into space. Stanley slaps him on the shoulder.]

STANLEY : Hey, Mitch, come to!

[The sound of this new voice shocks Blanche. She makes a shocked gesture, forming his name with her lips. Stella nods and looks quickly away. Blanche stands quite still for some moments—the silver-backed mirror in her hand and a look of sorrowful perplexity as though all human experience shows on her face. Blanche finally speaks but with sudden hysteria.]

BLANCHE : What's going on here?

[She turns from Stella to Eunice and back to Stella. Her rising voice penetrates the concentration of the game. Mitch ducks his head lower but Stanley shoves back his chair as if about to rise. Steve places a restraining hand on his arm.]

BLANCHE : [*continuing*] What's happened here? I want an explanation of what's happened here.

STELLA : [*agonizingly*] Hush! Hush!

EUNICE : Hush! Hush! Honey.

STELLA : Please, Blanche.

BLANCHE : Why are you looking at me like that? Is something wrong with me?

EUNICE : You look wonderful, Blanche. Don't she look wonderful?

STELLA : Yes.

EUNICE : I understand you are going on a trip.

STELLA : Yes, Blanche is. She's going on a vacation.

EUNICE : I'm green with envy.

BLANCHE : Help me, help me get dressed!

STELLA : [*handing her dress*] Is this what you—

BLANCHE : Yes, it will do! I'm anxious to get out of here—this place is a trap!

EUNICE : What a pretty blue jacket.

STELLA : It's lilac colored.

BLANCHE : You're both mistaken. It's Delia Robbia blue. The blue of the robe in the old Madonna pictures. Are these grapes washed?

[*She fingers the bunch of grapes which Eunice had brought in.*]

EUNICE : Huh?

BLANCHE : Washed, I said. Are they washed?

EUNICE : They're from the French Market.

BLANCHE : That doesn't mean they've been washed. [*The cathedral bells chime*] Those cathedral bells—they're the only clean thing in the Quarter. Well, I'm going now. I'm ready to go.

EUNICE : [*whispering*] She's going to walk out before they get here.

STELLA : Wait, Blanche.

BLANCHE : I don't want to pass in front of those men.

EUNICE : Then wait'll the game breaks up.

STELLA : Sit down and...

[*Blanche turns weakly, hesitantly about. She lets them push her into a chair.*]

BLANCHE : I can smell the sea air. The rest of my time I'm going to spend on the sea. And when I die, I'm going to die on the sea. You know what I shall die of? [*She plucks a grape*] I shall die of eating an unwashed grape one day out on the ocean. I will die—with my hand in the hand of some nice-looking ship's doctor, a very young one with a small blond mustache and a big silver watch. "Poor lady," they'll say, "the quinine did her no good. That unwashed grape has transported her soul to heaven." [*The cathedral chimes are heard*] And I'll be buried at sea sewn up in a clean white sack and dropped overboard—at noon—in the blaze of summer—and into an ocean as blue as [*Chimes again*] my first lover's eyes!

[*A Doctor and a Matron have appeared around the corner of the building and climbed the steps to the porch. The gravity of their profession is exaggerated—the unmistakable aura of the state institution with its cynical detachment. The Doctor rings the doorbell. The murmur of the game is interrupted.*]

EUNICE : [*whispering to Stella*] That must be them.

[*Stella presses her fists to her lips.*]

BLANCHE : [*rising slowly*] What is it?

EUNICE : [*affectedly casual*] Excuse me while I see who's at the door.

STELLA : Yes.

[*Eunice goes into the kitchen.*]

BLANCHE : [*tensely*] I wonder if it's for me.

[*A whispered colloquy takes place at the door.*]

EUNICE : [*returning, brightly*] Someone is calling for Blanche.

BLANCHE : It is for me, then! [*She looks fearfully from one to the other and then to the portieres. The "Varsouviana" faintly plays*] Is it the gentleman I was expecting from Dallas?

EUNICE : I think it is, Blanche.

BLANCHE : I'm not quite ready.

STELLA : Ask him to wait outside.

BLANCHE : I...

[*Eunice goes back to the portieres. Drums sound very softly.*]

STELLA : Everything packed?

BLANCHE : My silver toilet articles are still out.

STELLA : Ah!

EUNICE : [*returning*] They're waiting in front of the house.

BLANCHE : They! Who's "they"?

EUNICE : There's a lady with him.

BLANCHE : I cannot imagine who this "lady" could be! How is she dressed?

EUNICE : Just—just sort of a-plain-tailored outfit.

BLANCHE : Possibly she's—[*Her voice dies out nervously.*]

STELLA : Shan we go, Blaoche?

BLANCHE : Must we go through that room?

STELLA : I will go with you.

BLANCHE : How do I look?

STELLA : Lovely.

EUNICE : [*echoing*] Lovely.

[*Blanche moves fearfully to the portieres. Eunice draws them open for her. Blanche goes into the kitchen.*]

BLANCHE : [*to the men*] Please don't get up. I'm only passing through.

[*She crosses quickly to outside door. Stella and Eunice follow. The poker players stand awkwardly at the table—all except Mitch who remains seated, looking down at the table. Blanch; steps out on a small porch at the side of the door. She stops short and catches her breath.*]

DOCTOR : How do you do?

BLANCHE : You are not the gentleman I was expecting. [*She suddenly gasps and starts back up the steps. She stops by Stella, who stands just outside the door, and speaks in a frightening whisper*] That man isn't Step Huntleigh.

[*The "Varsouviana" is playing distantly.*]

[Stella stares back at Blanche. Eunice is holding Stella's arm. There is a moment of silence—no sound but that of Stanley steadily shuffling the cards.]

[Blanche catches her breath again and slips back into the flat with a peculiar smile, her eyes wide and brilliant. As soon as her sister goes past her, Stella closes her eyes and clenches her hands. Eunice throws her arms comforting about her. Then she starts up to her flat. Blanche stops just inside the door. Mitch keeps staring down at his hands on the table, but the other men look at her curiously. At last she starts around the table toward the bedroom. As she does, Stanley suddenly pushes back his chair and rises as if to block her way. The Matron follows her into the flat.]

STANLEY : Did you forget something?

BLANCHE : [*shrilly*] Yes! Yes, I forgot something!

[She rushes past him into the bedroom. Lurid reflections appear on the walls in odd, sinuous shapes. The "Varsouviana" is filtered into a weird distortion, accompanied by the cries and noises of the jungle. Blanche seizes the back of a chair as if to defend herself.]

STANLEY : [*sotto voice*] Doc, you better go in.

DOCTOR : [*sotto voce, motioning to the Matron*] Nurse, bring her out.

[The Matron advances on one side, Stanley on the other, Divested of all the softer properties of womanhood, the Matron is a peculiarly sinister figure in her severe dress. Her voice is bold and toneless as a firebell.]

MATRON : Hello, Blanche.

[The greeting is echoed and re-echoed by other mysterious voices behind the walls, as if reverberated through a canyon of rock.]

STANLEY : She says that she forgot something.

[*The echo sounds in threatening whispers.*]

MATRON : That's all right.

STANLEY : What did you forget, Blanche?

BLANCHE : I—I—

MATRON : It don't matter. We can pick it up later.

STANLEY : Sure. We can send it along with the trunk.

BLANCHE : [*retreating in panic*] I don't know you—I don't know you. I want to be—left alone—please!

MATRON : Now, Blanche!

ECHOES : [*rising and falling*] Now, Blanche—now, Blanche—now, Blanche!

STANLEY : You left nothing here but spilt talcum and old empty perfume bottles—unless it's the paper lantern you want to take with you. You want the lantern?

[*He crosses to dressing table and seizes the paper lantern, tearing it off the light bulb, and extends it toward her. She cries out as if the lantern was herself. The Matron steps boldly toward her. She screams and tries to break past the Matron. All the men spring to their feet. Stella runs out to the porch, with Eunice following to comfort her, simultaneously with the confused voices of the men in the kitchen. Stella rushes into Eunice's embrace on the porch.*]

STELLA : Oh, my God, Eunice help me! Don't let them do that to her, don't let them hurt her! Oh, God, oh, please God, don't hurt her! What are they doing to her? What are they doing? [*She tries to break from Eunice's arms.*]

EUNICE : No, honey, no, no, honey. Stay here. Don't go back in there. Stay with me and don't look.

STELLA : What have I done to my sister? Oh, God, what have I done to my sister?

EUNICE : You done the right thing, the only thing you could do. She couldn't stay here; there wasn't no other place for her to go.

[*While Stella and Eunice are speaking on the porch the voices of the men in the kitchen overlap them. Mitch has started toward the bedroom. Stanley crosses to block him. Stanley pushes him aside. Mitch lunges and strikes at Stanley. Stanley pushes Mitch back. Mitch collapses at the table, sobbing.*]

[*During the preceding scenes, the Matron catches hold of Blanche's arm and prevents her flight. Blanche turns wildly and scratches at the Matron. The heavy woman pinions her arms. Blanche cries out hoarsely and slips to her knees.*]

MATRON : These fingernails have to be trimmed. [*The Doctor comes into the room and she looks at him.*] Jacket, Doctor?

DOCTOR : Not unless necessary.

[*He takes off his hat and now he becomes personalized. The unhuman quality goes. His voice is gentle and reassuring as he crosses to Blanche and crouches in front of her. As he speaks her name, her terror subsides a little. The lurid reflections fade from the walls, the inhuman cries and noises die out and her own hoarse crying is calmed.*]

DOCTOR : Miss DuBois.

[*She turns her face to him and stares at him with desperate pleading. He smiles; then he speaks to the Matron.*]

It won't be necessary.

BLANCHE : [*faintly*] Ask her to let go of me.

DOCTOR : [*to the Matron*] Let go.

[*The Matron releases her. Blanche extends her hands toward the Doctor. He draws her up gently and supports her with his arm and leads her through the portieres.*]

BLANCHE : [*holding tight to his arm*] Whoever you are—I have always depended on the kindness of strangers.

[*The poker players stand back as Blanche and the Doctor cross the kitchen to the front door. She allows him to lead her as if she were blind. As they go out on the porch, Stella cries out her sister's name from where she is crouched a few steps up on the stairs.*]

[*Blanche walks on without turning, followed by the Doctor and the Matron. They go around the corner of the building.*]

[*Eunice descends to Stella and places the child in her arms. It is wrapped in a pale blue blanket. Stella accepts the child, sobbingly. Eunice continues downstairs and enters the kitchen where the men, except for Stanley, are returning silently to their places about the table. Stanley has gone out on the porch and stands at the foot of the steps looking at Stella.*]

STANLEY : [*a bit uncertainly*] Stella?

[*She sobs with inhuman abandon. There is something luxurious in her complete surrender to crying now that her sister is gone.*]

STANLEY : [*voluptuously, soothingly*] Now, honey. Now, love. Now, now, love.

[*He kneels beside her and his fingers find the opening of her blouse] Now, now, love. Now, love…*]

[*The luxurious sobbing, the sensual murmur fade away under the swelling music of the "blue piano" and the muted trumpet.*]

STEVE : This game is seven-card stud.

INTERNATIONAL BESTSELLER

THE POWER OF YOUR

SUBCONSCIOUS MIND

by Dr. Joseph Murphy

Pages	242
Size	8.5x5.5 inches
Binding	Hardback
Language	English
Subject	Self-Help
ISBN	9789387669222

'The Power of Your Subconscious Mind' has been a bestseller since its first publication in 1963, selling many millions of copies since its original publication. It is one of the most brilliant and beloved spiritual self-help works of all time which can help you heal yourself, banish your fears, sleep better, enjoy better relationships and just feel happier. The techniques are simple and results come quickly. You can improve your relationships, your finances, your physical well-being.

Dr Joseph Murphy explains that life events are actually the result of the workings of your conscious and subconscious minds. He suggests practical techniques through which one can change one's destiny, principally by focusing and redirecting this miraculous energy. Years of research studying the world's major religions convinced him that some Great Power lay behind all spiritual life and that this power is within each of us.

'The Power of Your Subconscious Mind' will open a world of success, happiness, prosperity, and peace for you.

OTHER HARDBACK BOOKS

- Abraham Lincoln by Lord Charnwood
  Biographies/Leaders, ISBN: 9789387669147
- Alice's Adventures in Wonderland by Lewis Carroll
  Children's/Classics, ISBN: 9789387669055
- Awakened Imagination by Neville Goddard
  Religion & Spirituality, ISBN: 9789389157185
- Be What You Wish by Neville Goddard
  Mind, Body & Spirit, ISBN: 9789388118163
- Becoming a Writer by Dorothea Brande
  Self Help/General, ISBN: 9789389157192
- Believe in Yourself by Joseph Murphy
  Mind, Body & Spirit, ISBN: 9789388118439
- Black Beauty by Anna Sewell
  Children's/Classics, ISBN: 9789388118262
- Civilization and Its Discontents by Sigmund Freud
  Social Sciences/General, ISBN: 9789388118279
- Feeling is the Secret by Neville Goddard
  Religion & Spirituality, ISBN: 9789389157208
- Gravity by George Gamow
  Sciences/Physics, ISBN: 9789388118705
- Great Speeches of Abraham Lincoln by Abraham Lincoln
  History/United States, ISBN: 9789387669154
- How to Attract Money by Joseph Murphy
  Self Help/Success, ISBN: 9789388118446
- How to be Filled with the Holy Spirit by A.W. Tozer
  Religion/Christianity, ISBN: 9789389157215
- How to Develop Self-Confi. and Pub. Speaking by Dale Carnegie
  Mind, Body & Spirit, ISBN: 9789388118286

Search the book by its ISBN

OTHER HARDBACK BOOKS

- How to Enjoy Your Life and Your Job by Dale Carnegie
  Self Help/General, ISBN: 9789388118293
- How to Stop Worrying and Start Living by Dale Carnegie
  Mind, Body & Spirit, ISBN: 9789387669161
- How to Win Friends and Influence People by Dale Carnegie
  Self Help/General, ISBN: 9789387669178
- Illust. Biography of William Shakespeare by Manju Gupta
  Biographies/Authors, ISBN: 9789387669246
- Madhubala by Manju Gupta
  Biographies/Cinems, ISBN: 9789387669253
- Meditations by Marcus Aurelius
  Non Fiction/Philosopy, ISBN: 9789388118781
- Mein Kampf by Adolf Hitler
  Autobiographies/Leaders, ISBN: 9789387669260
- My Experiments with Truth by Mahatma Gandhi
  Autobiographies/Leaders, ISBN: 9789387669277
- My Inventions: The Autobio. of Nikola Tesla by Nikola Tesla
  Autobiographies/Scientists, ISBN: 9789388118187
- Relativity by Albert Einstein
  Sciences/Physics, ISBN: 9789387669185
- Sense and Sensibility by Jane Austen
  Fiction/Classics, ISBN: 9789387669109
- The Alchemy of Happiness by Al-Ghazzali
  Religion & Spirituality, ISBN: 9789388118309
- The Art of Public Speaking by Dale Carnegie
  Self Help/General, ISBN: 9789388118477
- The Art of War by Sun Tzu
  Self Help/Success, ISBN: 9789387669321

Search the book by its ISBN

OTHER HARDBACK BOOKS

- The Autobiography of a Yogi by Paramahansa Yogananda
  Autobiographies/General, ISBN: 9789387669192
- The Diary of a Young Girl by Anne Frank
  Autobiographies/Memoirs, ISBN: 9789387669208
- The Dynamic Laws of Prosperity by Catherine Ponder
  Mind, Body & Spirit, ISBN: 9789388118194
- The Elements of Style by William Strunk
  Non Fiction/Skill, ISBN: 9789389157222
- The Game of Life and How to Play It by Florence Scovel Shinn
  Mind, Body & Spirit, ISBN: 9789388118316
- The Imitation of Christ by Thomas À Kempis
  Religion/Christianity, ISBN: 9789388118200
- The Knowledge of the Holy by A.W. Tozer
  Religion/Christianity, ISBN: 9789389157239
- The Magic of Believing by Claudie Bristol
  Religion/Christianity, ISBN: 9789388118217
- The Magic of Faith by Joseph Murphy
  Mind, Body & Spirit, ISBN: 9789388118712
- The Miracles of Your Mind by Joseph Murphy
  Mind, Body & Spirit, ISBN: 9789387669215
- The Origin of Species by Charles Darwin
  Sciences/Life Sciences, ISBN: 9789387669345
- The Path of Prosperity by James Allen
  Mind, Body & Spirit, ISBN: 9789388118323
- The Power of Awareness by Neville Goddard
  Mind, Body & Spirit, ISBN: 9789388118330
- The Power of Concentration by Theron Q. Dumont
  Self Help/General, ISBN: 9789388118224

Search the book by its ISBN

OTHER HARDBACK BOOKS

- The Power of Positive Thinking by Norman Vincent Peale
  Mind, Body & Spirit, ISBN: 9789388118729
- The Power of Your Subconscious Mind by Joseph Murphy
  Mind, Body & Spirit, ISBN: 9789387669222
- The Psychopathology of Everyday Life by Sigmund Freud
  Non Fiction/Psychology, ISBN: 9789388118231
- The Pursuit of God by A.W. Tozer
  Religion/Christianity, ISBN: 9789389157246
- The Quick and Easy Way to Effec. Speaking by Dale Carnegie
  Self Help/General, ISBN: 9789388118347
- The Richest Man in Babylon by George S. Clason
  Business & Economics, ISBN: 9789388118354
- The Science of Getting Rich by Wallace D. Wattles
  Self Help/Success, ISBN: 9789387669239
- The Seven Laws of Teaching by John Milton Gregory
  Self Help/General, ISBN: 9789388118460
- The Upanishads by Swami Paramananda
  Religion/Hinduism, ISBN: 9789388118774
- The World as I See It by Albert Einstein
  Non Fiction/Philosopy, ISBN: 9789388118248
- Think and Grow Rich by Napoleon Hill
  Self Help/Success, ISBN: 9789387669352
- Thought Vibration by William Walker Atkinson
  Non Fiction/Philosopy, ISBN: 9789389157253
- Wake Up and Live! by Dorothea Brande
  Mind, Body & Spirit, ISBN: 9789388118255
- Your Faith is Your Fortune by Neville Goddard
  Religion & Spirituality, ISBN: 9789389157260

Search the book by its ISBN